THE GLORY PATH

FROM GROWING UP AMISH AND BEING HEALED, TO HELPING OTHERS

STEVE LAPP

THE GLORY PATH

Copyright © 2012 Steve Lapp.

THE GLORY PATH
From Growing Up Amish and Being Healed, to Helping Others

Printed in the USA

ISBN: 978-0-9887287-0-7

Library of Congress Control Number (LCCN): 2012955548

All Rights Reserved. This book is protected by the copyright laws of the United States of America. This book may not be copied or reprinted for commercial gain or profit. The use of short quotations is permitted. Permission will be granted upon request. The author guarantees all contents are original and do not infringe upon the legal rights of any other person or work.

To contact the author or reorder:

Light of Hope Ministries

P.O. Box 567 | Ephrata, PA 17522

(717) 859-2614 | lightofhope777@yahoo.com

www.lightofhopeministries.com

CONTENTS

11	Chapter One **GROWING UP AMISH**
31	Chapter Two **THE ACCIDENT THAT CHANGED MY LIFE**
39	Chapter Three **HELPING OTHERS FIND HEALING**
63	Chapter Four **THE HEALING CENTER VISION**
77	Chapter Five **RUMORS, MISTAKES, AND MISUNDERSTANDINGS**
83	Chapter Six **THE BIRTH OF A NEW THING**
97	Chapter Seven **BLESSINGS OF HOPE OUTREACH**
109	Chapter Eight **INTERNATIONAL TRIPS AND THEIR PURPOSE**
119	Chapter Nine **BACK TO OUR ROOTS**
135	Chapter Ten **NETWORKING**

Special thanks to my wife Elsie for the work she contributed by editing this book, and to my brothers Jacob and David for helping to bring this story to reality.

FOREWORD BY LUKE WEAVER

Fifty years ago God put it on my heart to pray for the Old Order Amish. My prayer was that God would cause an awakening of His Spirit within the Amish Church so they would understand the Grace of God and receive the assurance of salvation. I also prayed that some of them would stay Amish as a witness to others in that church.

May, 2006 I met Steve Lapp and his family. I was thrilled to hear his testimony of his personal salvation and the healing he received. I was also blessed to hear how God was using him to pray for the sick and many were healed. Over the years since meeting Steve, I have observed him closely. I see him as a man who seeks God fervently and desires to do only what God tells him to do. Steve is a man of integrity.

I have seen him pray for people who have been set free from physical and emotional sicknesses. Steve is not in a hurry when he prays for people. He takes time with them until that person feels a release.

Steve Lapp communicates the true Kingdom of God in a clear way. He teaches how to wait on God and to actually hear God's voice. I am thankful I have lived long enough to see God move by His Spirit in the Amish Community.

Luke Weaver
Founding Pastor of Grace Chapel
Elizabethtown, PA

Luke and Edna Weaver

THE GLORY PATH

Steve Lapp is one of God's hidden vessels for the end-time harvest. He emerged out of the deeply segregated and religious system of the Amish, after God sovereignly touched his life and called him into the ministry of healing and reconciliation.

Today hundreds are coming to his ministry where they often experience immediate delivery of physical and emotional problems.

Steve, together with his brother Jake, stand alone in their dedication and service to the Lord. To compromise is not in their vocabulary. The misunderstanding and rejection that often comes their way only serves to advance the Gospel of the Kingdom with power, as they continue in their deliverance ministry.

Beyond this, Steve and Jake have been actively involved in the ministry of reconciliation among the Amish, Mennonites, and the body of Christ at large, that now spans three continents.

I have had the blessed opportunity to cross paths with Steve a number of years ago, where we have developed an unshakable covenant to walk together as we work in tandem to restore broken relations throughout our fractured Anabaptist people globally. Without a doubt, his ministry in the great end-time harvest has only begun.

Ben Girod
Bonners Ferry, Idaho
www.anabaptistconnections.org

Steve exudes boldness to do those things he believes God has spoken to do. Mixed with this boldness is a desire to see "his Amish people" become all that God intended for them to be.

Coming from the strong bonds of Amish family, he seeks to walk as an 'Ambassador of Reconciliation' even toward those who have rejected and shunned him.

I count it a privilege to have walked with him in Lancaster, Europe and Iraq.

Bob Doe
Executive Director of Light of Hope CSO.
Lancaster, PA

I am blessed to walk out the last few years with Steve Lapp, and the team at Light of Hope. We have shared the last six years of our lives together. We have learned to walk out the character and the nature of Christ, and transforming a group of people into all that God has created them to be.

By reading this book, your life will be transformed, and you will have the ability to get to know Christ better. I can highly recommend this book

THE GLORY PATH

because it will be a real blessing to everyone who reads it and it will transform their lives.

Pastor Mel Weaver

Grace Chapel

Elizabethtown, PA

Chapter One

GROWING UP AMISH

ON THE FARM

I was born on August 14, 1970, and was raised on a dairy and hog farm in New Holland, PA. Later on we also had produce and greenhouses. I was the oldest of ten children and had lots of responsibilities around the farm as I grew up.

We farmed with horses and horse drawn equipment. I enjoyed working in the fields. I also enjoyed grinding and mixing feed.

People have asked us over the years, "Isn't it hard to grow up Amish? Did you miss not having electricity? Did you really feel ripped off by not having a lot of this stuff?"

While growing up there wasn't another option for us. Therefore, it wasn't hard for us to live this way.

People would ask us if we use candles to light our houses. We did not use candles. We would use propane lights. I would say most Amish people's living rooms are just as bright as if they had electricity. In many ways it is not as hard as most people think, on the cultural side of things, because that is what we were always used to.

The Amish have a way of figuring out new ways to do things. Due to the fact that we could not use electricity, we had to figure out a new way to operate without modern conveniences. This causes the Amish to become very creative.

SCHOOL YEARS

I went to a one room parochial school, where we had grades 1-8 in the same room. I was one of seven boys in my grade (there were no girls). I believe we were a real challenge for our teachers. I give special thanks to my teachers, because I can now see that they had a huge impact in shaping my life for the future.

In first grade I was the only Amish boy in a room full of Mennonites. I can see that God was setting this up, to give me a heart to see reconciliation between the Amish and Mennonites.

TEENAGE YEARS

When I was 14, I started working as a hired boy for my grandmother and uncle on their farm.

When I turned 16 it was time for me to go with the Amish youth group. Because I went to school with the Mennonites, I would have rather gone with the Mennonite youth group than the Amish youth group at that time.

From age 16 - 18 I worked at a welding shop where we fabricated sawmill equipment. When my brother Jake turned 16, he started helping me at the welding shop.

When I was 17 I started courting Elsie Mae Zook. On our first date Elsie went to get milk out of the refrigerator and spilled it all over the floor. I was kind enough to clean it up for her.

When I was 18, Jake and I both started working at a fencing business as fence installers. We learned a lot of teamwork and delegation principles while working at this fencing business.

At 18 years old I was baptized by sprinkling in the Amish church and I had an experience with God at that time. I had been born again at 11 years old, while doing a mailbox Bible club program as a child.

THE GLORY PATH

On November 13, 1990, I got married to Elsie Mae Zook. Elsie and I were both 20 years old at the time.

OUR FAMILY

Steve Lapp—August 14, 1970
Elsie Mae Lap—August 29, 1970

—CHILDREN—

Elizabeth—August 28, 1991
Lydia Ann—May 20, 1993
Ivan—December 4, 1994
Jacob—March 3, 1997
John—March 3, 1997
Elsie—August 29, 1999
Eli—December 10, 2001
Isaac—January 23, 2004
Sadie Mae—November 17, 2005
Benjamin Allen—July 9, 2008
Mevin Jay—July 23, 2012

IN THE BUSINESS REALM

After I was married I was still working at the fencing business, but now instead of installing fences, I worked in the shop as a shop foreman. Later on I moved into the office and was working in accounting as well as dispatcher for the fence installation crews. As time went on I had an opportunity to become a part owner of the fencing business which brought on a new set of challenges. I believe this was a part of shaping the future for where God was taking me.

In the five years after we were married, while I was working at the fencing business, we were blessed with two daughters and a son. Our oldest daughter Elizabeth, was born on August 28, 1991. Our second daughter Lydia Ann was born on May 20, 1993, and our son Ivan was born December 4, 1994.

MOVING TO INDIANA

In the spring of 1995 my wife and I travelled with my parents and siblings to look at a farm that was for sale in Williamsburg, Indiana where a new Amish settlement was starting. By this time we had three children and when I saw the farmland I felt the tug on my heart to raise my family on the farm.

After returning to work and the challenges that I was facing at the time, I began to dream about moving to Indiana.

Dad bought the farm and told me that we could buy 80 acres of it to build on if we want to. We decided to take up this offer.

In October 1995 we moved to Indiana. At this time there were 16 Amish families living there. We formed close friendships with these people because most of us moved away from friends and family when we left Pennsylvania.

We started building our barn out in the middle of a soybean field. We built a dairy barn that could hold 41 milking cows.

LIVING IN A POLE SHED

Before we moved we built a pole shed for equipment storage. We used a section of the pole shed for temporary living quarters. Once we got over the fact that we were living in a pole shed it was actually a pretty neat place to live!

This is what my wife Elsie wrote:

My dad designed the blueprint for the living quarters in the pole shed. He never got to see our home in Indiana, because he died of cancer six weeks after we moved. We were traveling to Pennsylvania every two weeks to visit him. The night he died, most of us were outside watching a beautiful sunset. Within two hours after he died, the house was filled with family, friends, and people from the church. This was our first experience with death in the family and it was touching to see how the community reached out to my mother and the rest of the family. Mother still had seven children living at home.

We had plans to build a house once we had enough money saved to do it. That never did happen.

(Note: 17 years and four families later there are is still a family living in the pole shed that we built in 1995.)

On March 3, 1997, we were blessed with identical twin sons named Jacob and John. We didn't know until ten days before they were born that we were having twins. They were born at home.

My life was changed from working at an office job, to getting up every morning and milking the cows, getting the horses harnessed and working long days in the fields. All the field work was done with horses. We had engines built on some of the equipment to power the equipment, but the equipment was all pulled by horses.

FARM MEMORIES

Here is what my daughter Elizabeth wrote:

We moved to a farm in Indiana, in 1995. Everything was so different, as I sat there in the barn watching the action, the day our new cows came. They were dashing all over the dairy barn while some men tried putting them in their stalls. It was quite scary to my four year old eyes. Little did I know that pretty soon I would come to like these monsters very much!

Once when Dad and I were out in the barn, I asked him what the cows' names are. He told me what a few of them were, but a lot of them didn't have names yet. He pointed to one of the cows and asked me what I want to name her. I thought about it for a while and finally I replied, "Let's call her Jello." And with a grin I added, "Because I'm hungry for Jello." So that was it. From then on she was 'Jello'. I also named some of the other cows and calves throughout the years.

One day, we children didn't know what to do, and wanted an adventure. So we asked our parents if we may play with Beauty, one of our calves. She was so tame, unlike the other calves, and we wanted to lead her around with a rope, like a pony or dog or something. At first they didn't think that would be a good idea. What if she'd decide to run away? She could really hurt someone, especially a little child, but they decided we could try it. Dad and Mom helped us put a rope around her neck and lead her around until they were convinced she wouldn't harm us. We spent days pulling the poor calf all over the farm.

THE GLORY PATH

I remember one Sunday afternoon when we were playing outside we saw one of our cats fall in the manure pit. How terrifying! We ran as fast as we could to find Dad or Mom. When we told them what happened, they came to look at it for themselves. Dad climbed to the other side of the chain link fence and leaned in to get it while holding on to the unsteady fence. He had to lean in pretty far and it was frightening to watch. I couldn't help thinking, "What if he'd fall in too?" But soon he had rescued our cat and was safely on the other side of the fence. What a hero! Sad to say the cat didn't make it more than a few days in spite of our efforts in cleaning her up.

We children enjoyed going to our grandparents who lived only about a mile down the road. We were there one evening, almost ready to go to bed, when Dad came and told us, "You have two little brothers." I could hardly believe it, but sure enough when we came home Mom was holding two little babies. My twin brothers!

At one time we had mice in our house and I used to like running after them and killing them. I can still see myself with a broom in my hand trying to chase them out of their hiding places. Somehow that part of me changed over the years. I can't stand mice, dead or alive!

When we were little, my siblings and I loved riding along as Dad worked in the field. Sometimes we even rode in the empty bins on a corn planter or on top of a wagonload of hay. Other times we enjoyed running along behind and seeing if we could keep up. I have many good memories of living on the farm.

We also had some scary incidents. Like the time we were feeding the cows out in the woods and us children were sitting on the wagon, when suddenly something spooked

THE GLORY PATH

the horses and they started running for their lives. I fell off the wagon first and wasn't hurt badly, but my sister stayed on for a while before she fell off. She had lots of bruises from all the bouncing around on the wagon. But the worst part was that they couldn't find one of the smaller children at first. There was a creek nearby and we didn't know if he fell in there or where he was. Finally someone found him and he was fine.

And then there was the accident that changed our lives. We were almost finished baling hay for the day. I was up in the barn watching as the men stacked the hay when I heard a thud. I thought someone dropped a concrete block out the opening, but I saw the alarm on different peoples' faces and I knew something terrible had happened. I quickly found out that Dad had fallen and was lying on the ground. I ran downstairs and out to where he was. He was acting like it wasn't a big deal and he'll be fine, but when he went to the hospital, we found out that he wasn't fine, and he might never walk again. We stayed with our grandparents so that Mom could go to the hospital with Dad.

People came and helped out with the chores and brought food, etc. Mom took on the responsibility of the farm, along with our hired help, and life went on. While Dad was still in the hospital, Mom and us children would kneel in our living room and pray for him.

By the time I was seven or eight years old I helped milk the cows pretty regularly, But Mom did it in the mornings. One evening I was pondering what to give Mom for her birthday the next day. I don't remember if someone gave me the idea, or if I came up with it myself, but I told her I'll help milk in the morning instead of her.

Turns out, Mom had a beautiful baby girl on her birthday, so it worked out perfectly that she didn't have to go work in the barn. And, as you can imagine, that job kind of stuck for a while. I continued getting up early in the morning and helping with the milking for some time. I guess you could call it a prolonged birthday gift.

Dad gradually got better. He went from a wheel-chair, to crutches, to a cane, and finally could walk again. Praise the Lord! But he saw that he couldn't continue farming, so eventually we moved off the farm.

Elizabeth Lapp
Libby, Montana

INTEREST IN ANIMAL HEALTH

I always had an interest in keeping the animals healthy through proper nutrition. If there was some sickness in the cows, I would ask the vet if this was something I could learn to take care of myself. There came a time when I was doing most of my own animal health treatments.

Even though I enjoyed what I did I remember thinking there has got to be more to life than this.

This was written by my dad from his point of view.

THE BABY IS BORN

My wife, Lizzie (whom I married November 6, 1969) woke me early in the morning on August 14, 1970, and said, "Today we will have our first baby!"

At 8:00 AM, we went to the hospital. They took my wife away and told me where the waiting room was. It was a long forenoon. I did not see her again until after the baby was born. Steve was born at 12:30 PM, a big 9 lbs. 14 oz. baby. In the next 17 years the Lord blessed us with ten children (eight boys and two girls).

THE GLORY PATH

We lived on a 70 acre farm three miles north of New Holland, PA.

In the 1970s, we had dairy and hogs. In the 1980s, we added produce and greenhouses as our children's help increased.

The children went to school with three different groups of Mennonite children, which was a blessing. We had good teachers who taught them a lot of good biblical principles and inspiring songs.

The Amish have church services every two weeks. On the Sundays that we didn't have church, we had family Sunday school at home. This included reading the Bible in German and English as well as singing hymns.

In 1990, Steve got married and farmland in Pennsylvania was very expensive. I longed to have the children raise their families on farms.

In 1992, I went with a van load of friends on a trip to Kentucky, Indiana, and Wisconsin. I came home from that trip and told my family, "We don't all have to live in Lancaster County, Pennsylvania."

I was introduced to Wayne County, Indiana in 1993, and liked the area. We bought a 200 acre farm.

In 1995, we split the farm with Steve's and each of us built a cow stable and moved to Indiana. The next two years, we had the chance to buy the farms on both sides of us. That was a dream come true to imagine the boys farming in one neighborhood, working together, and sharing the equipment, etc.

SHATTERED DREAMS

In 1999, Steve fell out of the barn and crushed his pelvis. The doctor advised him to quit milking cows and move off the farm.

He studied how the body functions and people started coming to his house for treatments and also for herbs.

In 2003, David got married and took over the home farm. We had started a greenhouse business and we moved it off the farm to our own five acre corner.

Some years before I had a mishap and was dealing with a sore leg that did not want to heal. I went to Steve's house for prayer and herbs. At this time, we lived across the road from them.

Our children gave me a Life Application Study Bible and since I could not work full days, I studied the Bible and read other Bible related books.

In 2005 and 2006, six of our children and their families were excommunicated from the Amish church. We did not feel the excommunications were right or biblical, so it cost us our membership also.

This was very hard to accept, as I never dreamed I would not live and die a member of the Old Order Amish church. We have chosen to forgive and bless everyone involved, and move on with our life.

OVERCOMING

As I write this in November, 2012, we are again living in the same house we had lived in for our first 25 years of marriage. I am working in the greenhouses again that I built in the 1980s.

We are enjoying our walk with Jesus Christ and we are challenged with the forgiveness and unconditional love messages.

Some of my favorite Bible verses:

Therefore being justified by faith, we have peace with God through our Lord Jesus Christ.

—Romans 5:1.

THE GLORY PATH

And all things are of God, who hath reconciled us to himself by Jesus Christ, and hath given to us the ministry of reconciliation.
—2 Corinthians 5:18

Now then we are ambassadors for Christ, as though God did beseech you by us: we pray you in Christ's stead, be ye reconciled to God. For He hath made him to be sin for us, who knew no sin; that we might be made the righteousness of God in him.
—2 Corinthians 5: 20-21

Aaron Lapp
New Holland, PA

Chapter Two

THE ACCIDENT THAT CHANGED MY LIFE

On May 11, 1999 on a beautiful sunny day, we were at a school picnic and found out about a teenage Amish boy in the community that was involved in a farm machinery accident. He was airlifted to Miami Valley Hospital in Dayton, Ohio.

After the school picnic, we went home to bale hay and put it up in our barn. I thought I was living the Amish dream. My field work was ahead of schedule for probably the first time since we had started farming. The corn was all planted, we had an abundant crop of first cutting hay, and my future on the farm was looking great.

My brother and I were upstairs in the barn unloading the second load of hay when a field representative for our milk company came in the drive. On the end of the

THE GLORY PATH

barn there was an open door 11 feet off the ground. I had nailed a two foot high piece of plywood to keep the children from falling out. We had put the wagon tongue up onto this piece of plywood and stuck it out through the door so we could get the wagon load of hay closer to where we wanted to unload it.

When I heard the car coming in the drive I stepped down on the wagon tongue to see who it was and what he wanted.

When I stepped down on the wagon tongue the plywood kicked in at the bottom, tore loose from the nails that held it in place, and down I went head first.

I remember thinking on my way down that I cannot hit my head. Somehow I got my body twisted around and I ended up landing on my side. I knew immediately that something serious had happened.

When the ambulance crew arrived they started asking all kinds of questions to see if I was conscious.

The ride to the hospital was terrible. I was flat on my back on a solid backboard, I never knew we had so many pot holes on our drive, or that the road we had traveled on so often was this rough. I was in severe pain with every bump.

I was first taken to Reid Hospital in Richmond, Indiana, and I was later transferred to Miami Valley Hospital in

THE ACCIDENT THAT CHANGED MY LIFE

Dayton, Ohio. I ended up in the same room as the teenage Amish boy from our community that was injured in a farming accident the same day that I was.

HOSPITAL STAY

At the hospital the diagnosis came that my pelvis was crushed. It was in nine pieces and they would need to do an extensive nine hour surgery. A week later they put two metal plates and 21 screws into my pelvis to hold it together. They told me they cannot guarantee that I would ever walk again. They said I will probably need a hip replacement every seven years or so. (I have not had one yet!)

I was in the hospital for 13 days on some strong pain killers and I was still in intense pain. After I came home from the hospital, I still had to do therapy at home. My wife Elsie helped me with the therapy and I also had to get professional therapy at a local facility.

On August 29, 1999, (on my wife's birthday), we were blessed with a little girl. We named her Elsie, because she was born on her mother Elsie's birthday.

In October 1999, my brother Jake and his family moved to Indiana on the farm beside ours.

Also, in October of that year, one of my good friends, from Pennsylvania, died of a heart attack. We wanted to go to the funeral, but traveling 500 miles with a hip that was still hurting and an eight-week-old baby, looked like a big undertaking. We started calling taxi drivers, but no one was available to go on such short notice. While we were trying to decide what to do a van load of my Mennonite friends from Pennsylvania stopped in to visit us. They were on their way home from visiting friends and relatives in Missouri. Of course, one of the first things we asked them was if they had room to take us along to PA for the funeral. They said they had room for us to go along. They said they would go make a few other stops and be back for us in an hour.

By November, I was able to get around with only a cane.

STUDYING THE HUMAN BODY

When my accident happened I did not even know that I had a pelvis. When the doctors told me that I had a crushed pelvis I knew where it was because it HURT!

When I was in the doctor's office, he showed me some medical charts of the pelvis. I decided to get some medical charts for myself and study the human body. I studied where my pelvis was, what its functions were, and how it operated.

As I was studying the pelvis. I also studied the other bone structures of the body. I was so fascinated by what I

THE ACCIDENT THAT CHANGED MY LIFE

found that I decided to study the rest of the human body as well. I began to study the muscular system and then the nervous system.

I was especially intrigued by the autonomic nervous system and how the brain would give the commands throughout the body and everything was designed to flow together. If anything in the body is not functioning correctly, the whole body suffers. I began to see the parallel with the body of Christ. If there is any area in the body of Christ that is not functioning under the headship of Jesus, there is a problem.

A HIRED BOY WHO MADE A DIFFERENCE

We had a 15 year old hired boy who was a real blessing to us. Over the time I was in the hospital he stepped in and took over the farming as if it was his own. Without him there would have been a LOT more stress on Elsie and I.

MARKET IN CENTERVILLE

in the summer of 1999, I was helping my parents sell produce at a local farmers market. This was something I could do while being in a wheelchair.

THE GLORY PATH

In the spring of 2000, we started a farmers market in Centerville, Indiana. We sold fresh produce, dairy products, 'bent and dent' groceries, meats and cheeses, flowers, crafts, etc.

In the summer of 2000 we were planning on building a milk processing facility on my dad's farm. The milk prices were low and we thought if we could process our own milk and market it directly, farming could be more profitable. That did not happen then because there were a few neighbors that opposed it and we could not get county approval.

J&S FENCING

In the fall of 2000, we sold our farm and my brother Jake and I decided to go back to fencing. We had been working at a vinyl fencing business in Pennsylvania before we moved to Indiana, so we thought we could build fences and make a good living. We started a company called J&S Fencing in Centerville, Indiana.

HEALING WITH HERBS AND PRAYER

I was still having lots of pain, and it seemed like my healing should be progressing faster. I met some people who were telling me about using herbs, and the power of prayer. They prayed for me and I started taking

THE ACCIDENT THAT CHANGED MY LIFE

vitamins and herbs (especially lots of calcium). I noticed an immediate change for the better. I was not completely healed immediately, but I knew there was a shift and I felt better than I had for months.

As I continued my studies on the human body, I began to study the Bible on healing. The Bible talks about laying hands on the sick, and they shall recover. It also speaks about the power of prayer and using herbs when a person is weak.

I also began to understand that emotional healing plays a huge part in the physical healing. The Bible teaches many principles on blocks to healing. One of the main blocks to healing is unforgiveness.

As I searched my heart for unforgiveness, I realized that I was holding some unforgiveness towards a nurse at the hospital and some of the doctors.

Our son Eli was born on December 10, 2001.

THE GLORY PATH

Chapter Three

HELPING OTHERS FIND THEIR HEALING

HEALING FOR MY FAMILY

I discovered that healing is a gift from God. Some of our children were sick and I prayed for them, and I gave them some herbs. It was amazing how quickly they recovered. From this point forward I started praying for my family if they were sick.

A few of my brothers that lived close by started coming to my house when they or their children were sick. We would pray for them and give them herbs and they recovered.

OTHER PEOPLE COMING TO MY HOUSE FOR HEALING

As time went on, people started finding out about what was happening by word-of-mouth. They started coming to our house for prayer and for herbs. At first there were only a few, but as time went on, this started taking a lot of my time.

What began with a few people on evenings and weekends, very quickly mushroomed into a part-time job. This started interfering with our fencing business. I would work all day and meet with people till late at night and on weekends. I was getting so busy that I started dedicating one day per week to the healing vision, instead of the fencing business.

I had several nurses from the local hospital coming to my house for their own healing. They told me they wanted something better for their children.

Here is a testimony written by one of the nurses:

It was 2:00 AM when my four year old
daughter's alarming breathing woke me.
She had been itching with hives for the past

HELPING OTHERS FIND THEIR HEALING

two days. I cuddled her and could feel that the hives had spread to her chest and face. I was frantic when I realized that her body was covered in hives from scalp to feet.

I had been a registered nurse for nine years by this time. My husband was a registered nurse also. I took her to the nearby hospital. The doctor examined her and confirmed hives, an allergic reaction of some sort. He asked all the typical questions: "Had we changed laundry or bath soap? Did she wear new clothing? Had we got new cloth covered furniture or carpet?" Nothing had changed in our home or her environment. Baffled we went home with a bottle of Benadryl. Treating the symptom was not satisfying to us.

We had come to know Steve Lapp, an Amish man, who was beginning to treat sickness and disease by healing prayer and herbal remedies. We took her to see him in his home a few miles away. Steve worked with her and said she had been bitten by a spider on the back. He gave us a bottle of herbs and we went home.

We gave her the first dose and within minutes 1/3 of the hives were gone. My daughter had instant relief. A few hours later a second dose was given and again the hives disappeared. By the time the third dose was administered all the hives were gone.

My daughter is now a happy and healthy 11 year old. She has broken out in hives a couple of times since then and we quickly administer the same herbs that he had recommended before. It continues to work for her.

We are blessed to know Steve and witness his invaluable work. We still consult with him on our children's health.

Nicole Lainhart
Centerville, Indiana

HELPING OTHERS FIND THEIR HEALING

A picture of our herb supply.

MIRACLES THAT WERE HAPPENING ON A DAILY BASIS

Some of the miracles we were seeing healed on a daily basis were:

- broken bones
- severe trauma
  (black and blue marks with severe pain)
- pneumonia
- common colds
- backaches
- Alzheimer's
- blood clots
- kidney stones

- thyroid problems
- ... and many more!

BOY KICKED BY HORSE, WALKING THE SAME DAY!

One Sunday morning we were gathered together for church at an Amish family's home. The men were gathered together in the barn waiting until it was time to go into the house for the church services to begin.

As one of the teenage boys was helping people unhitch their horses, he got kicked in the leg by a horse. I was in the barn at the time, and I heard an audible 'snap'.

I hitched up my horse and drove to my house (about 5 or 6 miles away) to get some herbs for him. I spent a few hours that forenoon with him, praying for his leg and giving him specific herbs for his pain. I also gave him some herbs to help his bones heal quickly. By that afternoon he still had some pain but he was walking again.

TESTIMONIAL

In December 2003, our oldest daughter,
Katie was teething and had 105° fever.

HELPING OTHERS FIND THEIR HEALING

It was the first time she was sick. She had just turned one year old.

We took her to my brother Steve for prayer and herbs. We also gave her a vinegar bath. Soon she was much better, but we still stayed at their house overnight. The next day she was pretty much okay again.

We would have taken her to the emergency room if it wouldn't have been for Steve. Over the years since that, he has been our faithful counselor and friend.

Naomi King
Ephrata, PA

On January 23, 2004, our son Isaac was born. He was born at home, but due to complications Elsie had to spend a few days in the hospital after he was born.

THREE YEAR OLD GIRL FALLS ON HER HEAD

One evening, a couple from our church came to our home with their horse and buggy. Their three-year-old daughter had been doing knee hangs on a hitching rail and fell, landing on her head.

She was barely conscious when they came and I thought, "Wow, they must have more faith than I do, driving five miles with a horse and buggy, and expecting me to be able to help." She was white and limp, so we immediately started praying for her, and we gave her some herbs.

They were there for a few hours and by the time they were ready to go home she was smiling and asking to play with her doll.

OUR DRIVER'S ACCIDENT AND RECOVERY

In March 2004, our seventeen-year-old driver from the fencing business was in a bad car wreck. His friend was driving and lost control of the vehicle, hit an embankment, and flipped the car. He was thrown through the windshield and his friend was killed.

They told us he died three times on the way to the hospital. They used 60-80 units of blood the first 24 hours because of internal bleeding. He had severe

HELPING OTHERS FIND THEIR HEALING

trauma to the head, his body was severely swollen, his eyes were swelled completely shut, he was in a coma and not expected to live. He suffered from internal bleeding, a broken shoulder, a broken arm, a couple broken vertebrae, broken ribs, a broken leg, and his pelvis was in five pieces.

They had four units of blood running into his body when we got to the hospital. They flew in a special experimental drug from Cincinnati, Ohio to clot his blood. After they gave him this experimental drug, blood clots started showing up throughout his body, including his heart and lungs. They called the family together numerous times because of blood clots that they expected to be fatal.

Jake and I were in the waiting room with the family because he worked for us. We would press in and pray for the specific areas where the blood clots were presenting problems. There was a nurse in the family, so she knew where the problems were. This helped us to know what to pray for. Every time we prayed the report came back that the situation had improved. This dramatically increased our faith!

During the next few days, he stabilized a bit, so they decided to do some surgeries. They were operating on his stomach and they decided that, while they had him under anesthesia, they would put a pin into his leg and put his leg in traction.

After they put his leg in traction, they took an x-ray to make sure his bones were properly aligned. They came back and said, "That leg is not broken after all."

A few days later the doctors were planning to operate on his pelvis. We told his dad to ask them to take another x-ray before they start. They took an x-ray and came back and said, "We need to take another x-ray." They took another x-ray and came back and said, "We don't know what is going on, but his pelvis is not broken after all."

They had x-rays to prove that his leg was broken, then they had x-rays to prove that it was not broken after all. We did not hear another word about any of his other broken bones after that!

At one point he had severe pressure on his brain. We prayed against this and the next day they told us that their machine had been malfunctioning the day before. His brain pressure was back to normal.

They put him on kidney dialysis and the doctor said, "If he even survives, he will need to be on dialysis for the rest of his life." We prayed against that and within 24 hours they took the dialysis machine out of the room and we never saw it again.

By this time it was a few weeks after his accident and he was stabilizing to a certain degree. We were not going

HELPING OTHERS FIND THEIR HEALING

in to the hospital as regularly anymore, because it was spring time and we were busy building fences.

One day his dad called us and asked us if we could come to the hospital and pray for his son again. His dad said that he had pneumonia and it looked like they might still lose him.

We went to the hospital and I remember standing beside his bed praying, "Lord, how do you want us to pray for him?" (Up to this point we had very good success with pneumonia patients by using herbs in combination with prayer, but since he was in a coma we could not use any herbs).

The impression that I got was to put my hands on top of each other, about six inches above his body, and to pray. I told Jake to put his hands on top of mine.

As we were praying, suddenly there was a whoosh of power that flooded through our bodies. He started flopping around on the bed. The alarms started beeping and the monitors were reacting. He started coughing really hard and several nurses came running into the room as we hurried out the door.

We had to sit down and get a drink of water, because we were very weak in the knees and pretty shook up. I had never experienced this much power surge through my body before, but Jake had once been shocked by a faulty 220 volt electric outlet, and he said the experience was comparable!

The next morning his dad called us and said, "You won't believe this, but his pneumonia is completely GONE!"

This was a huge faith booster for us because up to this time we had been using herbs in combination with prayer, but since he was in a coma we were unable to give him any herbs.

We realized that we don't always have to understand what God is going to do. Our job is to be obedient to what God asks us to do, and leave the rest up to Him.

After being in a coma for five weeks, he woke up and had no idea of all the things that he had gone through.

The last I heard he was back to work with only a few limitations to what he can do. Keep him in your prayers because I do not believe God is done with him yet!

OUR INTRODUCTION TO THE DEMONIC REALM

In December 2004, we visited a friend at a mental facility. He was unexpectedly released that day. We invited him and his wife to go home with us and spend a few days at our house.

HELPING OTHERS FIND THEIR HEALING

They accepted the invitation and went home with us that night. We spent a few days together, sharing testimonies, studying spiritual principles, and working through some issues that he was dealing with.

One night we (Elsie and I, Jake and Nancy, and this couple) were in deep discussion on spiritual matters, and discussing the power of God, when a demon manifested in him. His face changed dramatically, his eyes became black and glassy, and his body became straight and stiff. I said his name and told him to come back! This demon replied in a deep, terrible, monotone voice, "He is NOT here, and he is NOT coming back!"

Coming from the Amish background, we had never experienced anything like this. I had read about it in the Bible about Jesus casting out demons, and I had read one account of a pastor who was doing a deliverance with a young man that had been involved in the occult. This pastor used the name of Jesus to cast out the demon.

In desperation, I said, "In the name of Jesus, come out of him." This demon just h-i-s-s-s-s-e-d at me. Well, that didn't help our fears any at that point. I tried it again, "In the name of Jesus, come out of him." I got the same results. I said it the third time, and the demon just hissed.

I knew it was not the name of Jesus that wasn't working. Somewhere we didn't have the authority that was needed to cast out the demon. There must be some area in our own lives that we had not fully surrendered to God.

When I got born again at age 11, I had made Jesus Christ my Savior, but I had never fully made Him my LORD. Up to this point, my focus was to do what the Amish church required. I had never fully surrendered everything to God.

We all fell down on our knees and our life flashed before our eyes. We started confessing everything we could think of that could be hindering us from being fully surrendered.

We committed everything to God (our wives, our children, our jobs, our properties, our possessions, and our own lives). We told God we would do whatever He asked of us. We were even willing to live in tents, if that is what He wants.

"JUST GET THIS THING OUT OF HERE!"

Then we started singing the song 'Gott ischt die Liebe' (translated 'God is Love'). While we were singing that song, the demon left, and the man asked, "Do you think I'm back?"

After he came back to his senses, he told us that he heard that deep demonic voice coming out of his own mouth, but he had absolutely no power to do anything on his own. He said, "It felt like I had one foot in hell while it was happening."

HELPING OTHERS FIND THEIR HEALING

This was our introduction to the demonic realm!

A while later God reminded us that He had kept His part of the bargain, were we going to keep our part? The answer was YES!

LEARNING ABOUT EMOTIONAL HEALING

People continued to come to our house for healing. We were able to help them with spiritual healing and with physical healing. However, we realized that there was an aspect about emotional healing that we did not understand.

In February 2005, we took the opportunity to attend an intense five day course on emotional healing. This opened our eyes to understanding the emotional needs of people. During that week we experienced emotional healing for ourselves and learned the principles of helping other people get set free.

The healing ministry exploded after this, but Jake and I decided that we needed to pull back the healing ministry, and focus more time on fencing. We thought we had to do this to bring in more finances, but the Lord had other plans. Almost immediately, it seemed like we were getting a lot less new leads for jobs.

The anointing had shifted, and it seemed like no matter how hard we tried, fencing could no longer be our primary focus. We now had to rely on the profits we made from selling herbs, and the contributions that we got from the people that were coming to our house for healing.

THE DRAWING TOGETHER OF OUR FAMILY

In the spring of 2005, there were five of us brothers, with our families, that started getting together on a very regular basis. We would get together almost every night. We would sit in a circle, holding hands and praying or singing. Sometimes we would read and study the Bible.

One day we were introduced to the concept of breaking generational curses. We read in the Bible that generational curses and iniquities can pass on for three or four generations. As we were discussing this idea, we talked about how most of us struggled with this certain weakness in our life. We also realized that our mother struggled with the same thing as did our grandmother.

We decided this must be one of those generational curses. We prayed to break the curse and immediately there were children, from a few different families, in three or four different rooms in the house, that woke up crying and vomiting. They had been sleeping soundly before that.

HELPING OTHERS FIND THEIR HEALING

Even though it was not an exciting thing to clean up the mess, we were excited because of the power of God that we had experienced.

The Bible also talks about generational blessings that are passed on to a thousand generations! This is awesome because as we get rid of the generational curses, we can experience the generational blessings that God wants to release.

Over this time we were seeing miracles to the extent that there was nothing keeping up part. Two of the families were milking cows twice a day. They would milk their cows in the evening and get together with us almost every night (sometimes until the wee hours of the morning).

COUPLE FROM PENNSYLVANIA COMES TO INDIANA FOR HEALING

in the spring of 2005, a couple came from Pennsylvania, because the wife had been struggling with a lot of negative feelings and illnesses. As we were working with her, she started talking about memories of abuse that happened in her childhood.

As she was talking about these memories, her body began to release cellular memories and to react the way that it would have reacted back when the original memories were created.

THE GLORY PATH

When she was a little girl, somebody had beat her up and whacked her across the face. As she was dealing with these memories, her face began to swell up and her jaw twisted to one side and one of her eyes swelled shut. She had a hard time speaking because her mouth was contorted. She also had to have her arm in a sling for a few days while her body was going through the healing that it needed.

All this happened right before our eyes. It helped us to understand the necessity of healing the emotional wounds instead of stuffing them or ignoring them.

Here is a testimony in her own words:

Five months after my husband and I were married I became ill. After doing all we knew to do we ended up in the emergency room on a Saturday evening. I was told I have the flu and was put in a room for further diagnosis. Sunday evening we were told I had appendicitis and they would be operating the next morning.

HELPING OTHERS FIND THEIR HEALING

They finally operated Monday afternoon (roughly 36 hours after my appendix had burst). I did not recover as expected and spent three nightmarish weeks in the hospital. When I was finally able to go home, I had lost all trust in doctors and hospitals and never wanted to go to either one again.

A little while later Jake and Nancy came to Pennsylvania from Indiana. They talked of how Steve was helping sick people with prayer and herbs.

I was instantly intrigued, because I knew I could not go through life without becoming sick again. Whenever Jake and Nancy came to Pennsylvania, we spent every minute with them that we could. It always felt like we could never get enough of them. I will always remember what Jake said just before they left. He said, "We are only a phone call away."

THE GLORY PATH

By this time they were beginning to connect physical illness with emotional pain and going to the root of the emotions for healing which was what I needed. At this point I was a young mother, and all my dream castles had crashed at my feet. As a girl I had used fantasies to escape the harsh realities of life and now those fantasies had been exposed as nothing but air.

Those phone calls to Indiana became my lifeline as Steve and Jake helped me sort through the rubble and find the little girl hiding under all the crumbled dreams, still clinging to them for all she was worth. After finding me they helped nourish me back to life and pointed me to fulfillment in Christ.

Those phone calls were the beginning of hours, weeks, months, and years of sorting through pain and confusion. I grew up in a wonderful Amish home and have many fond memories of my childhood, but there

HELPING OTHERS FIND THEIR HEALING

were circumstances that were out of my parents' control and knowledge that caused parts of me to shut down and hide.

Often it would feel like we were getting nowhere but Steve would remind me that it was as if we were cleaning a skyscraper. I would clean one floor then get on the elevator and go to the next floor. When I opened the door at the next floor it looked exactly like the floor I had just been on but it really was another level higher.

Often in the middle of things I would cry out to God, "There has got to be a better way." There is no way everyone can take hours and hours like this to find the healing they need. And praise God there is a better way.

God has, through experience, revelation, and study, given Steve and Jake many keys and enabled them to build a bridge that people can quickly cross from hurt to healing. I praise God for the journey He has taken me through and I praise God for the bridge.

There is no doubt in my mind that, had it not been for those phone calls and the help I received from Jake and Steve, I would be mentally ill and very dysfunctional. And had it not been for the bridge God has helped them to build I would still be struggling.

Just recently we were talking about moments when suddenly you look at your life and you think, "Is this actually my life?" Steve remarked that at that moment another part of you is probably waking up and peeking out. He recommended saying, "Hello, yes, this is your life. Welcome!"

Interestingly enough, the next day I was sitting on the rocker rocking our eighteen-month-old daughter and watching our five-year-old play

HELPING OTHERS FIND THEIR HEALING

when suddenly I thought, "Is this really my daughter?" So I said, "Yes, it is. And look here, these are your babies. Aren't they beautiful? Welcome." Instantly I felt a rejoicing within myself. In an instant, suddenly, there was an awakening, a healing, the crossing of a bridge.

And the journey continues. I still have much to learn but the author of my story, the Lord Jesus Christ, will finish the work He has begun in me. I will always be grateful to God for placing Steve and Jake in my life and I will always be grateful to Steve and Jake for being willing vessels. I will always be grateful that they are willing to be pioneers and bridge builders. Thank you Steve. Thank you Jake.

Barbie Fisher
Ephrata, PA

THE GLORY PATH

Chapter Four

THE HEALING CENTER VISION

In the spring and summer of 2005, we were having many people coming to our house for healing. There were van loads of people coming from Pennsylvania to Indiana for a few days, and sometimes up to a week at a time. We were experiencing miracles on a regular basis.

This is a picture of the house where a lot of miracles were happening!

TAKING THE VISION TO THE NEXT LEVEL

We had people telling us that we need to take the healing vision to a new level. We needed a building that we can work out of, so my family could have some privacy again. This facility would operate a lot more efficiently than doing everything in our house (up to this point I was working out of our house). We had people help us to draw up plans for a healing center. We had commitments of $300,000.00 to build this healing center.

The building was going to have:

- 3 counseling rooms,
- 8 motel rooms fully furnished,
- a kitchen,
- laundry room,
- waiting room,
- an herb store,
- an office,
- a full basement large enough for meetings

This facility was designed to be able to expand when the need arises. We had a vision to have a place where people can come to for spiritual, physical, mental, and emotional healing. This was to be a place where people could come and stay for a few days, weeks, or even months, while

THE HEALING CENTER VISION

they received the healing that they needed in order to be able to function again in their own home. This facility designed to provide the care needed for complete whole body healing.

We had the blessing of the local Amish community to move ahead with getting a healing center started. We had the bishop's approval, we had a blueprint (and still do), we had state approval, we had septic approval, and we had a public hearing coming up with the county to get final approval and it looked very promising that this (County approval) would not be a problem.

We had the building site staked off, and the process was moving ahead very rapidly, when suddenly everything came to a screeching halt, and all of our dreams and visions of having this healing center were shattered.

Because of a misunderstanding, the Amish community called a meeting (that we were not invited to) to discuss the situation. Some of the influential people in the community decided that everyone would be better off without a healing center, and we were not allowed to proceed.

It was a terrible blow for us because we thought we had full support from the community before we started planning this.

Note: There is now a produce auction on the exact spot where we had plans to have this healing center, and the layout of the building is almost exactly as we had planned it.

HOLY SPIRIT WEEK

In July 2005, we had a week of pressing in for more of God. This was a time when we did only the bare necessities, of what needed to be done, as far as work was concerned. We would get together all day and all night.

My brother David had hay laying all week that was ready to be baled, but he felt it was more important to be with the group. It was nice and sunny all week. On Monday of the following week they baled the hay. That next winter, when they took forage samples, his feed salesman told him he never saw such a high quality hay sample.

Later in the week there was a van load of Amish people visiting us from Pennsylvania. Everyone was seeking a deeper level of breakthrough. We were seeing healings but knew there was more.

On Friday afternoon of that week, I was laying on the edge of the bed, when suddenly I fell out of the bed, and onto the floor. I started speaking in tongues, and had no idea what was happening. I knew it felt right, but we had never experienced anything like it, and we had no

THE HEALING CENTER VISION

teaching about it. I didn't know until about half a year later what was happening that day.

On Friday evening of that week the bishop stopped in and said that the church leaders want to have a meeting with us on Saturday morning.

That evening we decided to have a campout, in my brother's meadow, in the clearing in the woods. Everyone gathered together and went out to the meadow. This was in a quiet peaceful spot surrounded by trees on all sides. There was a beautiful creek flowing through the woods, on a still, moonlit night.

We started a huge campfire. The flames of the campfire were shooting 15 to 20 feet high. There was no wind and the smoke was going straight up.

We spent the evening enjoying God's creation. Some of the people were awake all night.

Early in the morning, just as the sky was showing forth the first signs of morning, there was a small breeze that picked up the red embers of our campfire, and dumped them down over the top of us. It was to the point that we were discussing that it was like we were being baptized by fire.

Shortly after that, there was this one tree, that every leaf on this one specific tree started shaking and rustling. All the other trees around it were calm and there was no breeze. This lasted for approximately 20 seconds, then that tree stopped shaking, and a tree behind us started up. Then the second tree quit and a third tree started shaking. Then the third tree quit and it went back to the first tree again. The three trees were like a triangle around us. By this time God had our full attention! This was WAY OUT OF OUR BOX. We had never experienced anything even close to this before!

A little while later, there was a cloud that started showing us distinct pictures. This cloud would expand and show us a picture, then it would go back together and come out another picture. First we saw what looked like the ultrasound of an unborn baby. Then we saw what looked like an x-ray of an unborn baby. We could see the baby's spine and ribs, and the mothers spine and ribs.

After that we saw Jesus hanging on the cross. Then Jesus was hanging on the cross holding a baby in his arms. Then Jesus kissed the baby. After this I am not sure what order they were, but we saw a few more pictures. We saw Moses holding up the Ten Commandment tablets, palm trees blowing in the wind, a light house, and a few others.

This was a cloud in the sky that we saw with our own eyes. It was like God was showing us a PowerPoint slideshow in this cloud in the sky. Everybody in the group (five or six families, including the children)

THE HEALING CENTER VISION

saw it. Even the van driver that brought them from Pennsylvania to Indiana saw it. A few years later we met this van driver again, and he commented about his experience that morning.

Around 9:00 that morning, the ministers had a meeting with us. The meeting consisted of the leaders telling us that we need to stop the healing ministry. They told me I was not allowed to pray for people or sell herbs anymore.

I had a vision of Abraham laying his son Isaac on the altar. I felt like God was asking me if I am willing to offer up my 'Isaac' (my healing vision), because He has greater plans for me.

While we were meeting with them I broke out shaking all over again and speaking in tongues. There was absolutely no way I could stop it. The bishop told my wife that she needs to get help for me.

That afternoon the people that were at our house for the week, left to go back to Pennsylvania.

After this, there were people coming to my house begging me that I would pray for them. They told me that they would not tell anybody if I prayed for them, but I was attempting to be obedient to what the leaders were asking of me.

OUR TRIP OUT WEST

That next week we had to cancel all the appointments that were already scheduled for that week. It was very difficult to tell the people that we were not allowed to help them anymore. We felt the need to get away from everything and sort through the shock we had received.

We decided to take a family vacation and go to the Grand Canyon and Yellowstone National Park. This trip was a highlight for our family. An event that we still look back to with fond memories.

When we got to the Grand Canyon, we were struck in our hearts how vast and how big God actually is.

At Yellowstone National Park there was a big herd of buffalo crossing the road in front of us. We had to wait about half an hour until they were all gone. Some of them came right up to the motorhome.

At one place we were going up the mountain side where there was a steep cliff on the one side, and a sheer drop off on the other side. There was no way for any of us to get out of the motorhome because the road was so tight. When we got back to where we started, we saw a sign that said, "No trucks, RV's, or buses beyond this point, small cars only." We realized we were not supposed to be on that road with the motorhome, but we had missed the sign.

THE HEALING CENTER VISION

The trip out west, as remembered by Katie Ann (Jake and Nancy's daughter)

When we were no longer allowed to pray for people, we went on a trip out west. We went to the Grand Canyon. My mom was scared when I went down the trail a little bit. It was creepy! After a while, there were no guard rails on the side. If I would've tripped and fell, I would've fallen down, down, down.

We went through Texas, Utah, Arizona, and New Mexico on the way to Yellowstone National Park. We had a hayride in Texas and they had the song 'Old McDonald had a Farm' playing all the way.

When we got to Yellowstone National Park, we saw a big herd of buffaloes, two coyotes, and a bear. We also saw the Old Faithful Geyser. It was so beautiful.

This was the best trip I was ever on.

Katie Ann Lapp
Ephrata, PA

SAYING "NO" TO PEOPLE IN NEED

July to October 2005 was a very difficult time in our lives. We had people coming to our door asking for help and begging for us to pray for them. It was hard enough for me to understand why I was not allowed to pray for them. It was even harder to explain to the people in need why I had to turn them away.

Finally in October, after praying and seeking the Lord on this difficult situation, We felt convicted that it wasn't right that we weren't using our God-given talents.

As we were praying we got the Scripture verse in James 4:17 that talks about if we know to do good and don't do it, that to us it is sin.

Therefore to him that knoweth to do

good, and doeth it not, to him it is sin.

James 4:17 KJV

THE HEALING CENTER VISION

I made a public statement in church that I would not be able to turn away people in need anymore. From now on I will help people to the best of my ability. The church then put my wife and I on a probation period because they perceived I was being disobedient.

THE MIRACLE WITH MY NEPHEW

In November 2005, as my brother David was finishing up his chores, he heard a commotion behind him. He looked around in time to see one of his cows jump on the back of his 15 month old son. He quickly ran over and dragged his son out from underneath the cow. When he picked his son up he realized that his son was obviously hurt, and gasping for breath.

We had been experiencing miracles on a daily basis, so his first thought was, "I need to get him prayed for."

David ran a quarter-mile across the field and came running into the house where we were all gathered. He plopped his son, who was hardly breathing, on my lap, and said, "He needs prayer."

I immediately knew this was serious. I did not know the extent of his injuries, but I did know that he was hardly breathing, and also that a 1200 lb. cow jumping on the back of a 15 month old child don't go together very well.

We all gathered around in a circle holding hands and started praying. As long as we stayed focused on praying or singing for him, he would sleep. If we got off focus or the circle of prayer was broken, he would immediately wake up and cry.

We started noticing that if anyone in the circle disconnects their hands, he would wake up and cry. So we tested it a few times and every time someone disconnected their hands, he would wake up and cry. The Lord showed us the power of group unity.

After five hours of intense prayer, singing, Bible reading, and occasionally testing if he wakes up when we disconnect our hands, he finally went on sleeping. So we knew we had a breakthrough!

The next day he still was a little sore, but two days later he was climbing up on the furniture and playing again as if nothing had happened.

DAUGHTER SADIE MAE IS BORN

On November 17, 2005, we were blessed with a daughter, and we named her Sadie Mae. She is our ninth child.

When Sadie Mae was two weeks old, Elsie and the baby got on a pony cart, and I pulled them over to Jake's house through the snow.

THE HEALING CENTER VISION

GETTING EXCOMMUNICATED FROM THE AMISH CHURCH

In December 2005, my sister Naomi was very sick and decided to come to our house for help, instead of going to the emergency room in the hospital.

When the Amish leaders found out that I was helping people again, (they knew that my sister had gotten better without going to the hospital) they told me I would have to promise not to help people anymore, or we would be excommunicated from the Amish church.

In January 2006, my wife Elsie and I were excommunicated.

In February 2006, Jake and Nancy, along with my sister Naomi and her husband Steve King were also excommunicated.

Chapter Five

RUMORS, MISTAKES, AND MISUNDERSTANDINGS

RUMORS

By this time there were a lot of rumors going around about us. I guess it probably was because we were doing some things that were out of the ordinary, and it was getting people's attention.

We will attempt to clear up a few of the rumors that we have heard.

- There was a rumor going around that we were sitting around and doing nothing except waiting until the end of the world comes. The truth is, there were lots of people that desperately needed help and we believe that God wanted us to be helping them.

- There was a rumor going around that we charged a man $5,000.00 for a prayer. The truth is, we were asked to come to someone's house, to pray for his wife who was dying of cancer. We were there numerous times to pray for her, and to support them. After a long battle, she ended up dying at their home, in the care of hospice. A while later her husband came to our house and gave us a $5,000.00 check. He wanted to support the ministry so that others could get help.

- There was a rumor going around that we were wife swapping. I have no idea who came up with this rumor or what they were basing it on, but it is absolutely not true. We all got a good belly laugh out of this one!

If you heard something about us and you don't know if it's true or not, ask us.

MISTAKES

In early May 2005, someone from Pennsylvania was taking a lady (who was mentally challenged) to a doctor in Tennessee. They decided to stop at our house in Indiana along the way.

RUMORS, MISTAKES, AND MISUNDERSTANDINGS

It was decided that my wife Elsie and I, and my brother Jake and his wife Nancy, would go along to Tennessee to meet this doctor.

Somewhere along the way, while we were on the way from Tennessee back to Indiana, the lady lost her medications. At that time we did not understand the dynamics of mental illness, so we weren't too concerned about it.

After we got back it was decided that this lady was going to stay with us and we would spend some time with her.

She stayed in Indiana for four months. We spent many hours ministering to her, singing, praying, scripture reading, and deliverance, and saw many miraculous breakthroughs. There were times when she was calm, cooperative, and pleasant to have around. There were also times when she would flip into another mode and she would get rough and violent where it took two or three of us to restrain her.

There were times when she would literally, audibly, call in demons. She would pull up a chair beside her and then she would pet them, she would call them by name, and actually carry on a one-sided conversation with them. If anyone sat on that chair while she was in that mode, she would literally freak out, and start to hit that person.

One day she came out of the bathroom completely naked. This was the last straw for us. We grabbed a blanket and threw it around her. We then grabbed a roll of net wrap and wrapped her up in that and tied her to the bed.

One night she was in a bad mood and was flopping around on the floor. In our ignorance, we reacted and restrained her to make her behave. There were a few of us holding her down when we noticed she was no longer breathing. By all appearances, she was dead.

We were praying and crying out to God. WE WERE DESPERATE! By all appearances we had murdered her.

I had visions of spending the rest of my life in jail, my children growing up without a father, and my wife spending the rest of her life at home without a husband.

After praying and crying out to God for a while, we gave up and we were sitting there in shocked silence. Reality had hit us full force. Nothing was working. WE WERE DONE!

We completely surrendered everything to the Lord. I said, "LORD, IT iS IN YOUR HANDS." We were willing to take responsibility for our actions and face the consequences.

Suddenly we noticed she was breathing again! SHE WAS ALIVE! God had done the "MIRACLE of MIRACLES!"

RUMORS, MISTAKES, AND MISUNDERSTANDINGS

We immediately broke forth into some serious singing, praise, and thanksgiving for a few hours after that!

To this day every time we hear the song, "How Great Thou Art," (a song we sang over and over again that night) we immediately go back to this specific moment in our life. It reminds us of the time when God showed up in His AWESOME GREATNESS, and backed up our mistakes with his awesome GRACE!

A few weeks later she went back to Pennsylvania. She is now at a facility that specializes on helping mentally challenged people.

We visited her a few times at this facility and she is always glad to see us.

Soon after this, we felt convicted and made a trip to Pennsylvania to apologize to her extended family for all the mistakes that we had made while ministering to her.

MISUNDERSTANDINGS

I am not sure what exactly caused us to be excommunicated. I believe it was a misunderstanding of the authority that the church has versus the absolute authority of God.

To my understanding Jesus is the head and the church is the Bride. To properly flow we need to keep the head in authority. If the church (the Bride) is not flowing with the head (Jesus Christ), there will be a problem to properly discern what God is doing.

Chapter Six

THE BIRTH OF A NEW THING

WHERE TO FROM HERE

In March 2006, we were at a meeting in Vincennes, Indiana. The speaker started prophesying to us. He was prophesying some radical stuff over us that week, but it was confirmation to what we had already been sensing in our spirits.

Throughout that year, these words were reconfirmed over and over again to us by many different people.

To date, a lot of what had been prophesied that year has already come to pass, and the rest of it looks much more possible than it did at that time.

THE MOVE BACK TO PENNSYLVANIA

In May 2006, we (Jake's family and our family) moved our families back to Pennsylvania, to Lancaster County where we had come from. We both rented houses in the Ephrata area about a mile and a half apart.

Up to this point we had been involved mostly with individual healing. As we continued our journey, we realized that individual healing is necessary, but to really make a big difference, it is also necessary to follow God's principles, and to help reconcile people groups and nations.

We got involved with the healing and reconciliation efforts that were beginning to happen among the Anabaptists. Our eyes were opened up to the need of global reconciliation among the whole body of Christ.

At this time I realized the studies that I had been doing on the human body were also relevant to heal the body of Christ.

HEALING OUR HEARTS CONFERENCE

In September 2006, we were involved with a conference at Grace Chapel in Elizabethtown, PA. This conference was called "Healing Our Hearts." The purpose of the conference was to heal any unforgiveness or bitterness that was in the hearts of the Mennonites and the Amish. And also to heal the rift that happened when the Mennonites and Amish split.

ISRAEL OCTOBER 2006

In the summer of 2006, Jake and I were at a tent meeting, and the speaker was sharing about a team that was going to Israel for a tour of the Holy Lands. Jake and I talked about it, and we both believed we were supposed to go along on the trip.

During the break, a man walked up to us and told us that he believed we were supposed to go on the trip to Israel. He handed us a blank check with a signature on it, and told us to use this check to cover whatever we still need when the time comes to pay for the trip.

On October 2, 2006, Jake and I were on our way to the airport, when somebody called and told us that a man had entered a one-room Amish schoolhouse in Nickel Mines, PA. He had taken some school children hostage.

When we got to the airport in New York City, there was news on all the TVs at the airport about the situation in Nickel Mines, PA. The gun man had shot ten Amish girls. Five of them were killed and five were critically wounded.

When we arrived at the airport in Frankfurt, Germany, the news was also on the TVs at the airport there.

Then when we arrived in Tel Aviv, Israel, the news was also on the airport TV screens there.

All over Israel, people were coming up to us and asking about the shooting and about the Amish. This gave us an opportunity to speak about forgiveness.

We spent eight days touring Israel. Jake and I got baptized in the Jordan River.

One of the security guards came up to the group leader and asked him, "What is different about your group? I work here, and I have seen many groups come here to be baptized, but I never saw this much energy in a group of people before."

He wondered what the difference was, so our group leader told him about the power of Jesus. The security guard said, "I want that."

The group leader shared with him the plan of salvation, and the baptism of the Holy Spirit. The security guard received Jesus into his heart, and got baptized immediately.

GLORY BARN MEETINGS

In December 2006 (Christmas weekend), we had three days of meetings known as "The Glory Barn." It went day and night in a barn in Palmyra, PA. It was in the middle of

THE BIRTH OF A NEW THING

the winter, 20-30 degrees, no heat, cracks around the side of the barn, and cold air coming in. People were wrapped in blankets, and sitting on hay bales.

There was teaching, ministry, worship, prayer, food, fun and fellowship. There were many people in and out over the weekend. Sometimes people would come late at night or early in the morning to help with night watch. People came to experience the presence and glory of God!

We were pressing in, praying, and standing in the gap for our friends and families who were still in the Amish church.

We had the main meeting in the upstairs of the barn. In the downstairs of the barn we had some toys and Bible videos for the children to watch. The farmer got someone to dump a load of shelled corn into an area for the children to play in. Sometimes they got really dirty.

There was a separate building where we had set up a cafeteria where hot food, coffee and tea were available. There was heat in this building, therefore, a lot of fellowship happened here.

There were a few hundred people that showed up throughout the course of the weekend. We had lots of food, and we had an awesome time.

Years later we had someone share at one of our meetings. They told us they re-dedicated their lives and were stretched and challenged way out of their comfort zone that weekend at the "Glory Barn." They are now missionaries to China. We had no idea until 2012, what had happened in their lives in 2006.

LIVING TOGETHER IN COMMUNITY

In January 2007, the Lord asked us to go into community living with four other families. We were to function as they did in the book of Acts where they had all things in common.

We have one checking account for the group. If there are any conflicts, we need to work them out as a team.

There are the five families that are now known as the: Light of Hope Ministries team.

- Steve & Elsie Lapp
- Jacob & Nancy Lapp
- Steve & Naomi King
- Aaron & Barbie Fisher
- David & Fannie Lapp

During the next few years there were a lot of issues that needed to be dealt with. This gave us a lot of training to learn how to function as a team.

THE BIRTH OF A NEW THING

GROUP PRAYER FOCUS

Over the years there was a prophetic friend who was teaching us how to listen to God. We would all sit in a circle and pray and ask God to speak to us. We each had a pen and paper and would write down what we believed God was telling us.

After a few minutes of silence, and everybody writing what they got, everybody in the circle would then take a turn to read what they wrote on their paper, and somebody would write it on a whiteboard. We would then discern together as a group what the corporate word was for the day.

It was amazing how often multiple people within the circle were hearing the same things and how it always seemed like there was a theme throughout the whole group for the day.

52 DAY "GLORY BARN 2007"

In the spring of 2007, we decided to do a 52 day "Glory Barn" starting on Good Friday and going through Pentecost Sunday. These meetings included 24 hours a day of prayer, worship, teaching, intercession, night watch, fellowship, food, and getting to know new people.

The first few weeks of the "Glory Barn" were at Grace Chapel in Elizabethtown, PA. From there, we moved it to Victory Christian Fellowship in Palmyra, PA for a few weeks. After that we spent the rest of our time at Woodcrest Retreat in Ephrata, PA. Even though we had our challenges, we had an awesome time!

This was repeated again in the spring of 2008 but this time we did all 52 days at Woodcrest Retreat in Ephrata, PA. In the Poplar View Pavilion.

HEALING OF A KNEE

In the summer of 2007, Aaron and Barbie Fisher went to the mountains for the weekend. Aaron was out mowing the lawn and his tractor mower got stuck in the mud. He got off the tractor and was trying to push it out of the mud. The tractor had a missing shield. He pushed against an exposed pulley with his knee. The engine on the tractor was running and the pulley cut a gash into his knee about three inches wide and fairly deep.

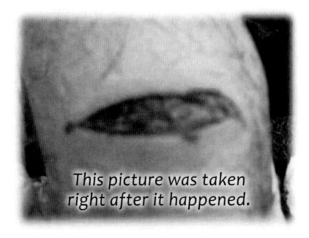

This picture was taken right after it happened.

THE BIRTH OF A NEW THING

They were out in the mountains about two miles from cell phone service. Barbie drove the two miles to where she had cell phone service again. She called me, wondering what they can do.

I advised them to get some raw eggs and peel the membrane off of the inside of the egg and put it over the wound. As the raw egg membrane dries, it pulls the wound together and allows it to heal. We have found that this works better than stitches. They did this and also prayed for the knee. Barbie later told me that it never occurred to her at the time to do anything other than to call me.

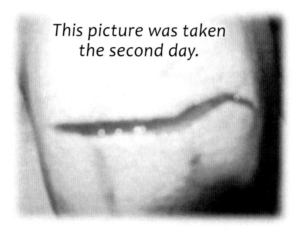

This picture was taken the second day.

The next morning when it was time to change the bandage and egg membrane, she had some reservations about taking the bandage off, for fear of what she would see. What a surprise when they took it off to reveal a beautifully healing knee!

THE GLORY PATH

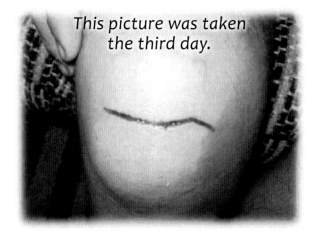

This picture was taken the third day.

A week later we met with a friend who is a medical doctor, and we showed him the picture of the knee, right after it happened. The doctor wondered how long ago it had happened. We told him it had been a week. He wondered if the person got stitches. We said he did not. He said it is probably pretty nasty and infected and it might be too late to put stitches in.

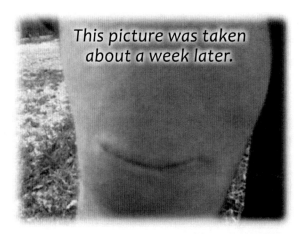

This picture was taken about a week later.

THE BIRTH OF A NEW THING

Aaron was with us, so he pulled up his pant leg and showed him the scar. The doctor was amazed. He said that having a cut right in the knee like that, it is hard to heal. This area of the knee is a high movement area, and it is very hard for stitches to hold something like that together. He told us if we would have taken him to the hospital, to get it to look as good as it did, they would've had to glue it, and that would have cost a few thousand dollars.

YARD SALE

In the summer of 2007, the ladies decided it would be fun to make a yard sale with some of the things in the attic and in corners that they weren't using.

Everyone worked together and we gathered trailer loads of furniture, dishes, household items, and all kinds of things. We had a huge yard sale for a few Saturdays.

Here is a picture of our yard sale.

THE GLORY PATH

APPLES, APPLES, APPLES

In October 2007, we had a need for some apples. We had gotten a few bushels off our own trees, but it was not enough for what we wanted to do. We wanted to make some applesauce for our families for the year.

One day a few of us got in a circle and prayed, "Lord, surely there is an unwanted tree of apples somewhere that we can pick." We also asked some of the neighbors if they know of any extra apple trees around the neighborhood that nobody was picking.

Aaron Fisher went to a prayer breakfast, and through that he got in touch with somebody that knew of an abandoned orchard in Harrisburg.

A developer had bought the orchard and they were preparing to tear out the trees and put houses in. There were parts of this orchard that would not be developed for a few years. This orchard had 15 acres of apple trees and we were allowed to go in and pick as many apples as we wanted.

We went to the orchard in Harrisburg with a van load of people and a trailer. We picked lots and lots of apples. We ended up making 954 quarts of applesauce, 100 quarts of apple butter, 225 quarts of apple pie filling, and 479 gallons of apple cider! We also dried a lot of apples, and ate apples to our hearts' content!

THE BIRTH OF A NEW THING

We went door-to-door selling apple cider and got all our expenses covered, and still had a few hundred gallons of apple cider left that we put into the freezer to enjoy for the next year.

There have been a few times in the last five years that we were praying for specific items, and God boosted our faith by giving us WAY more than we could ever imagine!

This is a picture of rows of apple trees in the abandoned orchard.

THE GLORY PATH

Chapter Seven

BLESSINGS OF HOPE FOOD OUTREACH

HOW IT GOT STARTED

In the summer of 2006, there were multiple families being excommunicated from the Amish church. Many of these families were in need of financial help, because of the separation from the way of life that was known to them. Some of them had lost their jobs because of what was happening in their life. There was a need to cut corners everywhere possible.

Aaron Fisher found out about this food pantry in Harrisburg that was giving out free food to people in need. We had never heard of this concept before. Why would anyone give out free food?

THE GLORY PATH

Aaron Fisher started going to Harrisburg with a plan to help at the food pantry and also bring some food along back. He was drawn to the environment of food distribution and people getting prayed for while they waited for food.

He started getting favor everywhere he went. People started to introduce him to their food suppliers and teaching him the logistics of running a food ministry.

At the December 2006, "Glory Barn," we got a box truck load of food, including two Gaylord bins of loose noodles. The person who gave us the food asked if we could use 22 bins of noodles. He said they didn't know what to do with them. We told him we couldn't take them at this point. (We found out later they threw them into a dumpster and sent them to the landfill).

Aaron passionately felt a need for a network to distribute the food that overwhelms one ministry, but would be able to bless many ministries if it were managed properly. There was also a need to utilize bulk foods and repackage them into manageable size packages. At first he was thinking someone else would do it, but then he realized God was asking him to do it.

There was a three car garage attached to Jake and Nancy's house that we turned into a food pantry. Someone gave us an 6' x 8' walk-in cooler, and a 4' x 10' walk-in freezer to use.

BLESSINGS OF HOPE FOOD OUTREACH

From there we started getting food from different ministries with a 15 passenger van. Later, we started using a 14 foot box trailer behind the van. Everything we got needed to be loaded and unloaded by hand. We did everything we could with the resources we had, going to different ministries for food and giving it to people we knew needed it.

A friend of ours introduced us to a local warehouse manager who blessed us tremendously with food. He gave us skids of bulk foods such as: bags of flour, sugar, cocoa powder, popcorn, oatmeal, and much more. Prior to that we had not been able to bake Christmas cookies because we could not afford to buy flour and sugar.

One time he gave us cereal, crackers, Oreo cookies, and candy. We were so excited, we were like little children in a candy store. Not only was it a blessing to receive the food, but we were also able to enjoy giving it to many other families.

One day we got a call from a trucker that was at a local truckstop. He had two skids of organic yogurt on his truck that he brought from Missouri. The supplier had put on two extra skids, and the store where he was taking it to refused to unload it because they had not ordered it.

The trucker was going to throw it into the dumpster at the truckstop, but the lady at the truckstop told him about us. Instead of dumping it, we were able to receive two skids of brand-new, organic yogurt. This was another awesome blessing that God provided for us!

HOW IT GREW

In the spring of 2009, we moved the food ministry to a larger garage. Immediately we started getting more food. We had many incidents where we were really hungry for something, so we specifically prayed for that item, and later we got lots of it.

One example of this was when we wanted a turkey for Thanksgiving, so we prayed for one. A little before Thanksgiving we got a bin with 60 or more turkeys. We were able to bless many families with these turkeys.

In late summer 2010, the food ministry went to a new level. We committed to give seven boxes of food a week to a local pastor to distribute. Barbie wondered if we would be able to do it. We had never before committed to distributing food on a regular basis. Up to this point we had only given when we had food to give.

Later that fall we were packing and sorting food outside and it was not very practical anymore because it was getting cold. We were praying about what to do. We knew we had to either push forward or pull back at this point. It was not going to work the way it was going at the time.

BLESSINGS OF HOPE FOOD OUTREACH

In December 2010, we moved the food ministry into a 3,600 square foot room. We told the owner of the building that we only needed half of the room, because it was too big for what we thought we needed. We now had a huge space to work out of, compared to what we had before.

First the vision was to pack boxes for ministries to distribute to their people. However, individual people wanted to get boxes as well. We realized that there are two aspects to the vision.

One aspect is outreach to individual families. The other aspect is to bring in truck loads of food and redistribute in manageable size quantities to ministries and outreaches.

Some warehouses send truck loads of food to the landfill, because they do not have someone to take the whole load. They do not want a bunch of small ministries to come pick out some of the food. They were looking for someone that would be able to take everything they had and distribute it from there.

Many small ministries serve 20-50 families, so they cannot receive tractor-trailer loads of one item, and still have storage space for a variety of foods. Also, they are run by volunteers who do not have the time and commitment it takes to build relationships with warehouse managers.

This created a need for a distribution center to warehouse the food and distribute it in manageable sizes, while networking with numerous ministries.

Within two months, there was such a supply of food coming in, that we had filled up the whole room. We had started with only half of the room because we thought it would be plenty big enough.

In July 2011, we sent a tractor-trailer load of food to an outreach at a Native American Indian reservation in Minnesota.

Food that was sent to the "White Earth Native American Reservation" this summer.

We almost gave up sending the food because they were not finding a trucker to take it out. At the "last minute"

BLESSINGS OF HOPE FOOD OUTREACH

a lady who was helping out at the outreach in Minnesota heard about the need for a trucker. She contacted her cousin who was a trucker, but he was not able to do it. However, he knew of another trucking company in Pennsylvania (approximately 15 miles from us). They were able to take the food out to Minnesota for them free of charge.

In November 2011, we setup "Blessings of Hope" as the name for the food ministry. We set up a board to allow the food ministry to operate as its own identity, as an outreach arm of Light of Hope Ministries.

Shortly after this, we moved to another warehouse at a temporary location. It was a 10,000 square foot room in the building. Again, it seemed like we had plenty of space for a few months, but that filled up very quickly as well.

We started receiving tractor-trailer loads of food. The network of ministries we worked with and the individuals we served continued to grow. God continued to supply the need.

In December 2011, we started to develop yet another aspect, which was disaster relief. In order to do this effectively, we need to dedicate an area in the warehouse to store non-perishable food items that will be ready to distribute immediately in times of disaster. Our goal is to be able to quickly distribute the food items in stock as soon as possible after the disaster happens. At the same time that this is happening, we are also contacting suppliers for additional products that are needed to fulfill the ongoing immediate needs.

In December 2011, we got a call from another ministry that had been contacted by a manufacturer that wanted to donate a large amount of Styrofoam cups. This ministry wanted some of the cups, but they were unable to receive everything that was available. They wondered if we were able to receive all of the cups and then they would receive only the amount that they needed.

In the next few months we received over 17 tractor-trailer loads of Styrofoam cups. A great deal of these cups were used for disaster relief in the months following.

WHERE WE ARE AT TODAY (IN 2012)

In May 2012, we moved into our current location. There were different things we were looking for such as dock levelers, built-in scales, controlled climate, and the right location.

The first nine months of 2012, we distributed an average of over 160,000 lbs. of food per month (this is more than one tractor-trailer load per week). At this point we are supplying churches, food pantries, halfway houses, street outreaches, rescue missions, and other food ministries with food, plus we have over 250 families getting food boxes on a weekly basis.

BLESSINGS OF HOPE FOOD OUTREACH

A picture of our food packing line.

In the summer of 2012, a few of the local social services and public schools called, asking if they could refer people to us who were in need of food.

There is a huge amount of food available. We have connections to fresh produce, milk products, dry products (flour, sugar, oatmeal, popcorn, salt, rice, etc.)

At this time we have a 38' x 58' x 14' cooler that was donated to us. We disassembled it and brought it home and are now storing it until we have the finances needed to get it set up and operating. We are currently using a reefer trailer as a cooler, until we can get the big cooler up and running.

At the time of this writing, November 2012, we are delivering many truck loads of food and other products for disaster relief as a result of hurricane Sandy.

AMERICAN FOOD STATISTICS

Here are facts that really opened our eyes to the need of having a food distribution network. According to National US statistics*:

- Nationwide, food makes up 17% of what gets sent to the landfill.

- According to a study done by the USDA, Americans waste almost 27 percent of all the food produced in the U.S. each year. That is the equivalent to one pound of food a day for each American.

- The average American household throws away more than 1.25 pounds of food each day.

- Each year, Americans discard more than 96 billion pounds of good food, and disposing of this waste costs our country over one billion dollars a year. If five percent was recovered, it could provide the equivalent of a day's food for four million hungry people; ten percent, eight million; and 25 percent, 20 million.

- Dumping food waste in landfills causes serious environmental damage. While food decomposes,

BLESSINGS OF HOPE FOOD OUTREACH

it lets off methane gas into the air, more than even carbon dioxide. By volume, food waste is the largest contributor to methane gas production. It also causes odor as it decomposes, attracting flies and vermin.

- According to research, about 96 billion pounds of food of the 356 billion pounds of edible food available. is squandered every year in the U.S., equaling a staggering $130 billion plus annually.
- Research has shown that the United States of America is the most wasteful country when it comes to throwing out and disposing of perfectly edible food.
- In 2008 nearly 50 million people in America, including almost one in four children, struggled to get enough to eat.
- One out of every six Americans are at risk for hunger.

Research was taken from http://www.planetgreen.com.

If you are interested in learning more information, if you want to stay updated on the Blessings of Hope food ministry, or you have a desire to become involved, we invite you to visit our our website:

www.blessingsofhope.com

You can also follow Blessings of Hope on FaceBook.

THE GLORY PATH

Chapter Eight

INTERNATIONAL TRIPS AND THEIR PURPOSE

SWITZERLAND, SEPTEMBER 2007

In September 2007, we were invited to go to Switzerland for an outdoor reconciliation meeting that was being headed up by multiple churches in Switzerland. The government of Switzerland had declared 2007 as "Tauferjahr" (the year of the Anabaptists).

Jake and I went with a team from Lancaster, PA to Switzerland for the three-day open air meeting with the Swiss Reformed Church, the Free Church, and the Anabaptists. It was a time of learning about some of the roots of the Anabaptist people. They had prepared for 3,000 people and I believe there were 4,500 to 5,000 people there.

This meeting was right beside the Trachselwald Castle, which is a castle where the Anabaptist people had been held prisoner during the time of persecution. We took a tour of the castle the day before the meeting started. It was very touching for us, as we thought of how it must've been to be a prisoner in this castle because of their faith.

We went to Sumiswald where Haslebacher was from. He was an Anabaptist who had been be-headed in 1571. He was one of the last Anabaptists to be killed for his faith. After they beheaded him, his head rolled over to his hat and laughed out loud, the sun turned blood red, and the town well started to sweat blood. An angel had come into his room at night and told him what would happen. Haslebacher then told the executioner that this would happen when they killed him.

INTERNATIONAL TRIPS AND THEIR PURPOSE

The whole region was so shook up by this incident that they quit killing Anabaptists for their faith. There is an account of this incident in the 'Ausbund' songbook, which is a songbook that the Amish use to this day.

We also went to the area where Jakob Ammon was born and raised.

IRAQ AND TURKEY, NOVEMBER 2007

In November 2007, we went to Iraq with a medical team. The leader of this team had asked us if we wanted to go along. He told us that the last time he was there, some doctors had asked him if he could bring some Amish people along the next time he comes, to teach them how to forgive.

These doctors had heard about the forgiveness message that went around the world, when the school shooting happened in Nickel Mines, PA. They said, "Our people need to learn how to forgive."

Jake and I told him that we would go along. As the time was getting closer for us to go. The tension was increasing between Turkey and Iraq. The PKK terrorist group had taken some Turkish soldiers hostage and they were hiding out in Iraq.

We had some people come to us and tell us that we should not be going to Iraq at this time. They did not believe it was safe. We told them, "If God wants us to go to Iraq, we are safer in Iraq than we are at home."

As we were flying into Mardin, Turkey, we had to circle the airport a few times because the airport was too small for another plane to land at that time.

As we were circling, I had a vision of a bear, flat on his back, with his four legs sticking up in the air. It was as if the spirit realm was saying, "I surrender to God."

We had a three hour taxi ride from the airport to the Iraq border. When we got to the border, we were interrogated by a military intelligence officer. After the interrogation, he told us the PKK terrorists had surrendered their hostages about three hours before that. We realized this happened at almost exactly the same time that we were circling the airport and praying over the region!

While we were in Iraq, we were at the mental health clinic, the prison, the boys orphanage, the girls orphanage, the women's shelter, the hospital, and the medical clinic.

Every so often, there were checkpoints along the way, where soldiers would stop the vehicles to check them out. At one of these checkpoints, the soldiers asked us to get out of the vehicle. When we got out of the vehicle, they asked us to have their picture taken with us.

INTERNATIONAL TRIPS AND THEIR PURPOSE

Iraqi soldiers wanted to have their picture taken with us.

SWITZERLAND AND FRANCE, NOVEMBER 2007

On the way home from Iraq, we made a stop in Switzerland and France to connect with some people that we had met in Switzerland a few months before.

We also went up into the mountains in Switzerland to look at the cave where the Anabaptists would go to hide and have their meetings. There was deep snow up in the mountains.

As we went up to the cave, we were trying to imagine how it would be to take a family up through the mountains, in the dead of the winter, to have a church service in the cave. I believe we underestimate the power of getting together as a group to worship.

This is the cave where the Anabaptists worshiped.

From there we went to the Alsace region of France. This was the region where the Anabaptists had moved to when they were being persecuted in Switzerland. We went to the place where the last meeting had happened to attempt to reconcile the rift between the Mennonites and the Amish.

At this spot Jake and I prayed and asked God for another chance to pick up the torch that the Anabaptists had dropped when they gave up on reconciliation.

INTERNATIONAL TRIPS AND THEIR PURPOSE

ISRAEL, NOVEMBER 2010

In November 2010, we were involved with a team of Anabaptists, led by Amish Bishop Ben Girod from Bonners Ferry, Idaho, on a trip to Israel. The mission was to meet with Jewish leaders, and apologize to them for the Anabaptists being silent while they were being persecuted during the Holocaust.

We acknowledged that Israel is God's chosen nation. The Word of God says, "He who blesses Israel will be blessed, and he who curses Israel will be cursed."

We met with Holocaust survivors, rabbis, the deputy mayor of Jerusalem, and we were also on Israeli TV and shared the message with the entire nation of Israel.

Following is the message that we shared with the people of Israel everywhere that we went:

TO THE NATION AND PEOPLE OF ISRAEL

On this day, we, representing the Anabaptist nation, humble ourselves and seek your forgiveness for our collective sin of pride and selfishness by ignoring the plight of the Jewish people and the nation of Israel. A tragedy, which has included the annihilation of six million Jews by the Nazis. Even in this hour, finds Israel surrounded by neighboring countries on all sides, bent on her destruction.

G-d, in His sovereignty, opened our eyes to the promise of Genesis 12:3 wherein He states; "I will bless those who bless you and curse those who curse you" As He has graciously opened our eyes to the gravity of this promise, we have corporately become deeply convicted of the reality that our collective ignorance of Jewish suffering is in fact nothing less than a historical rejection of the Jews: as well as a curse. To our shame, we have lightly esteemed you.

For this, we ask for your forgiveness.

Further, we publicly, and openly bless you and the people of Israel. We bless you as Abraham`s descendants according to Genesis 12:1-3. This promise given to Abraham, is

INTERNATIONAL TRIPS AND THEIR PURPOSE

about you, his descendants, for all future generations. We bless you because you have kept alive the faith in the one true G-d. We also honor you, as our parents in the faith.

At the core of our hearts, is a passionate desire to see the fulfillment of Amos 9:11-12. "On that day I will raise up the tabernacle of David which has fallen down, and repair its damages; "I will raise up its ruins, and rebuilt it as in the days of old. That they may possess the remnant of Edom, and all the Gentiles who are called by my name, says the Lord who does this thing." We bless your G-d promised borders as well—to the North, South, East and West, that you may prosper and fulfill your calling to the nations.

We pray for the peace of Jerusalem, according to the biblical injunction of Psalm 122:6.

In our brokenness and contrition, we shall not cease to hold our peace day or night, until He establishes Jerusalem, and makes Her a praise on the earth. Isaiah 62:6-7.

With unending love for Zion,
The Anabaptist Nation—your Amish and Mennonite brethren

Group picture of Israel trip, November 2010.

In November 2012, we plan to make another trip to Israel as a follow-up (by the time this book gets released this trip will be in the past).

<small>For more information about these trips, there is a FaceBook page set up: "Amish/Mennonite Apology to Israel." This page contains a three-part documentary made by one of our team members, and also news articles that were done as a result of our trips.</small>

Chapter Nine

BACK TO OUR ROOTS

ANABAPTIST BEGINNINGS

In 1525, there was a movement that broke off of the Reformed Church known as the Anabaptist movement. They were called "Anabaptists" because they were being re-baptized as adults for their confession of faith. They had been baptized before, but now they wanted to be baptized after they had fully surrendered to God.

This caused a great stir among the Reformed Church. The Anabaptist people were getting together for prayer meetings, Bible studies, and were aggressively sharing their faith.

The more they got persecuted, the more the fire of the Gospel spread. There were people being burned at the stake, drowned, and killed in various gruesome ways. They were also being banished from the region.

Some of their children got screws put into their tongues and under their fingernails because they refused to tell the authorities where their parents were.

Some of them could not bear the persecution (or to see their families being persecuted), so they compromised to save themselves and their families.

MUENSTER, GERMANY

In 1534, a group of Anabaptists got the revelation to establish a "New Jerusalem" on earth. They forcefully took over the city of Muenster, Germany, and forced everyone to be re-baptized, or to be banned from the city. This city had been a Catholic city, and all the Catholics were forced out.

With them assuming absolute authority, the enemy had the right to come in and disrupt what God had intended. The leaders were saying they "heard from God" and everyone else was expected to submit to what the leaders had heard.

With this doctrine, it opened a way for a "spirit of deception." They were preaching naked on the streets. They had multiple wives. One leader's wife spoke up at one point and he had her beheaded.

The Catholics that were banished returned with an army, to crush the rebellion. This led to a siege that lasted a few years. The Catholics finally broke through, and were so fed up by this time, that they killed all the men, women and children, except for the three leaders.

They put the three leaders in cages and paraded them all over Europe. After they had paraded them over Europe, they brought them back to Muenster.

Each of the three leaders were attached to a pole by an iron spiked collar, and his body ripped to pieces with red-hot tongs. One of the leaders saw the process of torturing done to one of the others, and he attempted to kill himself with the collar, using it to choke himself. The executioner tied him to the stake to make it impossible for him to kill himself.

After the torture, their tongues were pulled out, and then they were killed with a burning dagger thrust through the heart.

The bodies were placed in three cages and hung from the steeple of St. Lambert's Church and the remains left to rot. The cages are still hanging there to this day (November 2012).

Another group of Anabaptists looked at this situation and decided that it is not safe to "hear from God" or to be "led by the Holy Spirit." This created a cultural fear of the Holy Spirit. They decided to ONLY go by the written word of God and reject the Holy Spirit.

This episode in history distorted what God intended to do with the Body of Christ. God intended for people to hear His Voice, search out the Truth, and be led by the Holy Spirit.

THE ANABAPTIST COMPROMISE

By the 1650's, the Anabaptists became weary of persecution and tired of suffering. Something had changed, and they no longer carried that unquenchable passion (because of rejecting the Holy Spirit). They became inwardly focused to protect themselves, because they no longer had the fire to endure the persecution, or to reach out to others.

Because France had been in a 30 year war, their farmland had been devastated. The French knew that the Anabaptists were hard-working people and they wanted them to come to restore the land. They invited the Anabaptists to come to the Alsace Region of France, and offered them a written compromise. Some of the benefits of the compromise were:

- no persecution
- financial security
- social acceptance

Some of the consequences of the compromise were:

- they were not allowed to have public meetings
- they were only allowed to gather in small groups
- they were not allowed to share their faith outside their own group

The Anabaptists agreed to this in writing. After this they settled down and set their hearts to farming the land. They became known as the "silent in the land."

Because they accepted this compromise:

- they lost their power
- they became inwardly focused
- they gave up their inheritance

THE MENNONITE/AMISH SPLIT

In 1693, a Mennonite bishop by the name of Jakob Ammon, led an effort to reform the Mennonite church to include shunning, to hold communion more often, and other differences. After much impatience and frustration they decided to go their separate ways. (The followers of Jakob Ammon are known today as the Amish).

For more information on the Anabaptist history. I recommend the book *Unlocking Our Inheritance* by Janet Richards. Janet did an in-depth study on what our forefathers went through and put it into a book.

This book can be purchased through: Light of Hope Ministries, P. O. Box 567, Ephrata, PA 17522, or send an email to: lightofhope777@yahoo.com.

THE PRAYER WALK AND RUN

In July 2008, a team of people from France came to Lancaster County, PA, with the intent to break the curse off the people, and off the land. They also declared that the Anabaptists are no longer bound to the written compromise of being the "silent in the land."

The French team, and a group of people from Lancaster County, walked around the borders of Lancaster County, declaring new life among the Anabaptists.

This prayer walk took about a week, with teams of people walking different segments at the same time.

One of the groups that were prayer walking.

As the walk was nearing completion, the revelation came forth in a dream, to declare freedom and victory, by running around the county, along the same route that we had walked.

On July 26, 2008 at 4:00 AM on Saturday, we started out running, carrying a flag stating "Jesus ist Sieger" which is interpreted "Jesus is victorious." We had around 12-15 people with over half of them being children from the ages of 6-15 years old.

THE GLORY PATH

My son, Eli (age 6) running, carrying the flag.

We had a van full of people following the person that was running. One person would run with the flag in their hand until they got tired, then they put up their hand to signal for the next person to run. The van would then pass the runner and drop off the next person. The runner would run up to the relay person, pass the flag, and get back into the van while the next person would keep running with the flag.

After about 45 minutes of running everyone in the van was very tired. We realized that without Divine intervention, there was no way this was going to be completed. We were discussing the options of how we could continue. We prayed and the answer that we got was to go until everyone has given all they have to give.

BACK TO OUR ROOTS

Shortly after that two of the young guys from the French team showed up to run. The first one got out and ran over a mile! Then the second one ran a mile and a half! After that everyone in the van got a fresh wind and they all wanted to run again!

After a few hours the French boys had to leave, and we were wondering how it would go from here. Suddenly everyone in the van was able to run further than before. Soon after that a man showed up and ran five miles! The people in the van started getting anxious to run again.

Two people were in a car, shuttling people that wanted to run for short distances. They would take them from their vehicles to the van, and also map out the next turns for the runners, and schedule people to meet us along the way.

Running the victory lap!

After about 3/4 of the way around the county, there was a marathon runner that was planning to run ten miles. After he ran about six or eight miles, we came to the city of Columbia, where we met a mob of 50-100 people, that all wanted to run IMMEDIATELY! There was a sudden challenge of having too many runners rather than not enough.

At 1:30 AM on Sunday there were a group of 40 - 60 people all running together to declare the victory as we finished the run at 2:00 AM!

The total distance around Lancaster County is 147 miles, this was run in 22 hours, which is an average of 6.68 miles per hour.

On July 9, 2008. Our son Benjamin Allen was born.

TESTIMONIAL

I had been sick for many years. Gradually losing my physical and mental health, no longer able to function in daily life. I was spending around 75% of my time in bed.

BACK TO OUR ROOTS

My husband and I sought for answers in many ways over the course of the next years. Going to natural and medical doctors, and trying many nutritional supplements and diets, spending thousands of dollars, all to no avail.

The medical doctors all told me the same thing. All the physical symptoms that were manifesting in my body were rooted in the emotional and I needed to get help via counseling. I resisted it for some time, until a highly trained neurologist told me in a very kind but firm way that I would never get well if I did not accept that this illness was emotional and get help. He very emphatically told me I do not need medicine, but rather counseling. That day something changed inside me and I realize the doctor was right.

Life was increasingly becoming dark. My mental health was deteriorating to an even greater degree. My only hope was in Jesus, my Lord and Savior. As I spent hours lying on the floor,

THE GLORY PATH

in anguish crying out to Him for hope and healing, for direction. One day a loud and clear voice spoke to me in my bedroom and told me to fast for seven days. The spirit of the Lord told me that one day my health, physically and emotionally, would be restored, but first I would suffer many things. I had not had an experience like that before, nor have I had one since.

I began receiving counseling from Kenneth Kuhns, one of the ministers in the church we had just started attending. He ministered much hope and unconditional love into a life that was shattered and bleak, with no light at the end of the tunnel. Pouring hours of selfless agape love, Jesus love, and believing in me, when from human reasoning, there was no reason to believe. God really used him over the course of the next year to build a foundation of trust in my life, that would allow deeper healing to occur.

BACK TO OUR ROOTS

At the end of that first year I was again crying out to God from the depth of my pain and darkness, crying out in a way one only can when the situation is desperately beyond human help. Seeking his face through much fasting and prayer. After many days of this, God intervened in a sovereign way and one day my husband and I found ourselves sitting in the office of Steve and Jake Lapp, in Ephrata, PA. These were people who the day before we had not known even existed.

They told me right up front that in a sense, I would be their guinea pig. They had experience in working with people, but not much with people that were as severely mentally broken as I was. I was okay with that because I knew God had sent me. Thus began an intense journey of healing, with them walking with me over the course of the next few years, with my pastor and a previous counselor Kenny Kuhns still being involved to a degree.

THE GLORY PATH

As they began walking with me, I saw them with imperfections and places to grow like the rest of us, but with a passion and desire to give all for Jesus, to be Jesus hands and feet to a hurting world, in a way that we don't encounter that much in today's world. Laying down high dollar jobs at the Lord's direction, to begin a ministry of faith, not turning a broken hurting soul like me away. In spite of the fact that most of our finances have been poured into other avenues in previous years as we look for healing, in spite of the fact that they were having to live very sacrificially to keep on helping me. It is Jesus in us that enables us to do such things!

They, along with my husband and Kenny, believed in me many many times, when in the natural there was no reason to believe. Patiently teaching me truth about who I was in Christ, exposing Satan's work and the lies woven all throughout my being, walking with me through the terrible painful memories,

BACK TO OUR ROOTS

leading me to Jesus for his sweet healing. Pouring hours and hours and hours of truly selfless agape love into me. Loving me when I was very unlovable, losing much sleep during my darkest nights, and during my lashing out as the pain got out of control. Ever guiding me towards the light of Jesus, and who He said I was. Teaching me about the power of the words coming out of my mouth. Helping me to go to Jesus to change me from the inside out.

My life has changed dramatically, because God's servants were willing to be obedient. I am no longer bound to my bed, with unending sleepless nights, minutes ticking by as in eternity. No longer do I have a crushing weight of emotional pain in my bosom, no longer do I feel like I am constantly living on the brink of insanity, no longer do I endure seemingly endless nights filled with terror, but sleep the slumber of peace, with a thankfulness that comes from enduring years of sleepless nights.

My relationships are deepening as I am learning how to care for others. God is allowing me to reach out to others in their pain and brokenness. My marriage is going it in the direction I have prayed for many years. That I would be able to submit, to give my whole heart to my husband.

I am not out of the woods yet, but I know that He who has begun a good work in me won't quit till I'm free. He continues to heal, one piece at a time. There are days I'm still controlled by the past, but He is always faithful to move me through it and out on the other side. My desire is to pour my life into other broken hurting souls, to help them find freedom in Jesus Christ, according to his will, for the rest of my life.

Arie Schmucker
Middlefield, OH

Chapter Ten

NETWORKING

OPENING PRAYER FOR THE PENNSYLVANIA STATE SENATE.

Jake and I were involved with a prayer team that met every week to pray in Senator Greenleaf's office. We would usually be in his office, praying while the Senate was in session.

I was invited to open the Pennsylvania State Senate in prayer by Pennsylvania Senator Brubaker on May 7, 2008.

Me sharing at the Pennsylvania State Senate.

CHICKEN PIES FOR A FUNDRAISER.

In November 2008, we decided to make chicken pies for a fundraiser to support the ministry. We started out by getting our carrots that we had grown in the garden, and dicing them with paring knives.

We very quickly figured out that we were going to have to come up with a better way to do it, so we decided to use a French fryer to cut them the one way and use paring knives to cut them the other way. This worked for a while until someone got the idea that we can put the slices in the other way too, and use the French fryer to dice them.

The first day we made thirteen pies all day, plus prepared some stuff for the next day. In a matter of nine days we had made 2,000 chicken pies.

Chicken Pie

NETWORKING

The next year we made 8,000 chicken pies and sold most of them door-to-door, or set up at local stores. Doing this really got us out of our comfort zone because most of us were not salesmen.

By this time we had people asking for chicken pies, and every year after that we are making around 2,000-2,500 pies.

We now have a system in place that we can make and bake 2,000 chicken pies in less than a week. Thank you to all the volunteers that help make the pies.

TESTIMONIAL

I was raised in a home where both parents were just out of the horse and buggy Mennonite church. There was abuse and neglect all around. As I grew up I developed severe insecurities rooted in this abuse and neglect as well as not knowing who I was.

My parents separated on my eleventh birthday and my life seemingly spiraled out of control. I fully blamed myself for their separation and felt every bit of condemnation from extended family and the community.

Everyone claimed to have the answer and I believed most of them at first. I became so confused I wasn't even sure that God could fix it. I began rebelling with all I could. Threats and violence became a way of life for me.

Soon I was locked away in psyche wards and labeled "mentally unstable." Prescription pills were forced upon me and at the most I took seven in the morning and four in the evening.

I found a strong passion for history in the seventh grade and studied obsessively. History was my coping outlet. With very few friends and fewer people that I could trust I had found something that I could turn to and preoccupy my mind.

It was during this time that I found books on Sanskrit writings and incantations. At school I was constantly bullied and could count my

NETWORKING

friends on one hand. I was desperate for a way out. Reciting incantations gave me a power to strike back at the bullies.

At 16, I went to a boys' camp for 1 year and 4 months. Here I learned to control my temper, relate to other people, turn to God, and unfortunately, how to convince people that all was fine when it really wasn't.

Roughly six months after graduating from the boys' camp, I was turning away from God and rebelling again. I was in training for a prayer ministry and on fire for God when I got mixed up with a party crowd and smoking on the job. I asked for prayer support and was turned out like a leper.

I decided that if this was God, I wanted nothing to do with Him. Instead I turned to another party crowd that included pagans, witches and a deep connection to the occult. Several people taught me how to do certain rituals, incantations, and blood sacrifices. The most influential teacher would later turn on me.

From age 18 to age 25, I was a practitioner and rather good at hiding it. Very few people knew what I truly was.

At age 20, I lost my best friend to suicide. His death impacted me deeper than I could fully realize.

Around age 23, I became friends with a young man and got to know his wife as well. After he left her, she and I remained friends.

After several years of her praying and asking me to go to church, I agreed to go to church. What she didn't know is that I was going for a two-fold purpose.

Several pagan coven masters had asked me to infiltrate this church and bring it down. I was more than happy to try. After five short weeks of going to this Pentecostal church I responded to

NETWORKING

an alter call by rededicating my life to Christ and turning my back on the darkness I once served.

Everything I had worked seven years to build was torn apart in five weeks by the power of God's love. Satan had nothing real to offer!

From 12 years old until this point in my life I had attempted suicide around forty times.

Awhile afterwards a friend asked me to go with him in his semi truck for a week. I hesitantly agreed. That week I heard the names Steve and Jake Lapp so often I became convinced I had to meet them. At the end of the week I met them for the first time and had a roughly two hour deliverance session.

Ever since, I have been working with them to remove any remnants of my past life. And I am teaching others to identify and overcome it.

These two brothers and their ministry helped me overcome incredible obstacles and achieve a much deeper understanding of God, His Word, and what is expected of us Biblically.

After one year of counseling with them I met my wife and married her five months later. Our first child, a daughter, was born almost a year later.

Just before her birth, I received word that my old teacher was hunting me because I betrayed the ways he taught me. It never amounted to more than words. No one ever showed up or even talked to me.

We now openly and willingly serve God and continue an awesome friendship with Steve and Jake and all of Light of Hope.

Anthony Martin
Leola, PA

NETWORKING

MOVING INTO MOTOR HOMES

In April 2009, we had the sense that there is a need to connect with communities across America. My family and Jake's family moved into motor homes. Moving into motor homes enabled us to fulfill the vision of taking the families along when we went out to minister.

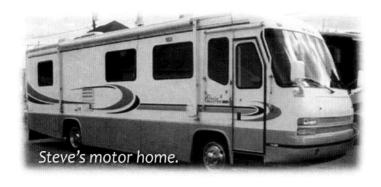
Steve's motor home.

My son Eli's story about our Florida trip:

Every year our family goes to Florida for the winter. In Florida we met lots of nice people. One of them was a trapeze trainer. She was teaching us children to trapeze. We loved it. She said we can do it anytime.

Another thing that was interesting was that we were playing basketball. My sister and my cousin were cheerleaders.

Eli Lapp
Ephrata, PA

TESTIMONIAL

Hardly knowing where to start, we will start at the time just before we met Steve and Jake Lapp and their wives in northern Indiana which was the year 2009.

At that time we were married twelve years and found ourselves trapped in the vicious grip of family, marriage, financial, and church struggles. We had no idea how to get out of it or repair what was broken. It was taking its toll on our children and it showed up in school with our oldest son getting into trouble.

NETWORKING

Not knowing what to do in the situation, I (Amos) said to my Dad, who was principal at the time, "We can't give our son something we ourselves don't have." Seeing this as an opportunity to help us he immediately told me that we need counseling. That hurt, but at the same time I knew there was some truth to it.

A few weeks later a cousin of mine called me and was all excited about these Amish Lapp brothers from PA that he met at a prayer meeting. And they drive motor homes! He went on to tell how they are helping people find freedom from all kinds of issues by praying to God then listen for Him to speak to you . In the course of the conversation I told him to get us three appointments without thinking or talking it out with my wife.

In looking back we can see that God was working.

I (Rhoda) was not impressed with that decision, and tried to come up with excuses for not going, but God was working in that too! By the way, I have many times since then thanked Amos for making those appointments!

Anyway as we were traveling to Indiana for our appointments, there was a spiritual battle going on, and by the time we came to Indianapolis we almost turned around and went back home. We didn't know about spiritual battles then. All we knew was that we were having these weird feelings, but we decided to go on.

When we got there, we were waiting for our appointments, when we saw these two Amish ladies come around the corner of the building with such radiant, peaceful expressions on their faces! We looked at each other and said, "These are not regular Amish people!" (We later found out they were Steve's wife Elsie and Jake's wife Nancy).

I (Rhoda) was having a terrible battle with FEAR! which was the first thing that Steve

NETWORKING

helped me with, which was only one of the many things that we worked through. And after three days we felt so liberated, having worked through layers of hurts and abuse.

Our happiness was very obvious, so much so that when Amos' mom saw him she asked in total surprise, "What have you done, you look ten years younger!" I (Amos) took that as an opportunity to share about our experience, but it was not well received. We were soon met with rejection from those that were the closest to us.

This all happened in May of 2009 and by the end of that year we were excommunicated from the Beachy Amish church and totally rejected by most of the people from church. This of course caused a lot of hurt, but through this, the Lapps taught us how to forgive these people as Jesus would. If it wouldn't have been for the Lapps teaching us about the love of

God, and the power of forgiveness, we would not be writing our testimony in this book.

We have been through some deep waters in the last three yrs. but God has been so faithful. God knows what He is doing, and we know it is for a specific reason that He has called us out, and let us go through these trials. Now we can look back and thank God from the bottom of our hearts for those trying times. We can truly say that they have made us stronger. AND TO GOD BE ALL THE GLORY!!!

Thank you Steve & Jake for caring!
Amos & Rhoda Chupp
Crofton, KY

Amos & Rhoda Chupp and their family

NETWORKING

TREE FALLING ON BROTHER JAKE'S MOTOR HOME

In October 2009, Jake and Nancy's motor home was destroyed by a tree falling on it. The barn was being painted at the time, so they had moved their motor home to a different spot for a few days. The painting crew was finished with the barn and they could move their motor home back to the original spot that evening. Before they got the motor home moved, the tree fell on it.

This picture is the outside of the motor home after the tree fell.

Here is how Jake and Nancy felt about this:

It was a very beautiful, wind still night before Halloween. We were on our way to a gathering. It

THE GLORY PATH

was a fun, fellowship, and food night. On the way there, nine-year-old Alvin felt like we shouldn't go. We weren't sure what we should do, but we decided to go anyway. We had a good time while we were there.

When we came home we went into the motor home and left our coats on until it warms up. All of a sudden, there was a crashing and banging, the camper was rocking, and in through the roof came a tree, close to where Jake was sitting (the tree was huge, about three feet in diameter). The tree fell across the two front seats and laid right on the horn. The horn kept on blowing until the battery was disconnected. We were all very scared when it happened.

We were parked at that spot because they were painting the barn that day. We were deciding if we want to move the motor home to its original spot that evening yet.

Earlier that day, Katie Ann was trying to turn the front seat around, but it did not move for her. If someone would have been sitting there, it would have been right where the tree landed.

Praise the Lord, that no one got hurt. We were all in the camper, including six children. We were getting ready to pray when the tree fell.

Later we saw the tree had twisted as it fell, and we believe there was an angel right beside it when it fell. It looked like the angel pushed the tree to the side, so that it would not fall on somebody. If it would have fallen straight down, it would have landed right where we were sitting at the time.

This picture is the inside view where Jake was sitting.

THE GLORY PATH

This was written by my daughter Elsie as she remembered it:

> It was the night before Halloween. Uncle Jake was home for approximately ten minutes when something very unexpected happened. They were parked along the drive for the night because someone was painting the barn.
>
> They just got home from a gathering, when a huge tree fell through the roof of their motor home! It landed on the horn! Good place to land. They all got out safely.
>
> The next morning we saw that the tree had twisted and that made it hit the front of the motor home. If it would have come straight down, it would have came down right where they were sitting.
>
> Earlier they were trying to turn the driver's seat around to sit on it but could not. I

NETWORKING

believe that there were angels with them, protecting them. PRAISE THE LORD!

Elsie Lapp
Ephrata, PA

This was written by Jake's son Alvin as he remembered the event:

It was the night before Halloween and our family went to a party. Before we went I felt like we should not go. But we went anyway and we had fun.

When we got back we all sat down to pray and a tree fell on the camper. It missed us all but the camper was totaled. When they looked at the tree they saw it had twisted, if it would not have twisted, it would have smashed my dad.

Praise the Lord!
Alvin Lapp
Ephrata, PA

"ADOPT-A-STREET" NEWARK, NEW JERSEY

In 2008, we met with a couple who were telling us about a program they were doing in Newark, New Jersey. In this program they were praying for streets of the city. The goal was to transform the entire city of Newark.

As we were speaking with them, we mentioned to them that they should get the worst streets adopted and prayed for first. They told us that nobody wanted to adopt the worst street. We volunteered to take that street, and later they asked us if we could adopt and pray for the entire neighborhood.

At the time they implemented this program, Newark, New Jersey was considered the murder capital of America. Immediately after launching the "Adopt-a-Street" program, the city went over a month without a murder. Before that they were used to having up to eight murders per day.

Today 100% percent of the streets in Newark have been adopted are being prayed for on a regular basis.

This model is spreading worldwide to other cities that are now also getting their streets prayed for on a regular basis.

For more information, go to: www.prayfornewark.org

NETWORKING

TESTIMONIAL

This is a testimony from one of my nieces (Jake's daughter) about Jake's wife (Nancy's mother):

In December 2010, one of my brothers was planning to go to Africa in a month. My grandmother found out about it, and asked angels to go with him. (She was having visitations from angels).

While she was shopping for her grandchildren for Christmas, she had a bad stroke. She was taken to the Emergency Room quickly.

When she was at the hospital, she told my mother and my aunt that there were angels there to take her away, but she told the angels that she wanted to spend one last Christmas with her children and grandchildren. At the Christmas dinner everyone, including all the little ones, told grandmother how much she meant to us.

In January 2011, grandmother died during the night.

Mary Lapp
Ephrata, PA

"UNDERSTANDING EMOTIONAL HEALING" CLASS

In the spring of 2011, we had a weekend of meetings at Grace Chapel in Elizabethtown, PA. During that time I shared a testimony about some youth that had experienced revival.

One of the older ladies came to me and asked me, "Why can't us older people have that?" I told her they can. They invited us to begin weekly meetings at Grace Chapel.

We started having weekly meetings called "Understanding Emotional Healing." These meetings were held in the forenoon, from 9:00 till noon. They were an open group type of meeting where anyone could come and be a part of it.

TESTIMONIAL

Here is a testimony of an older lady that was set free:

I am 64 years old and for the first time in my life, I feel free. I came from such an abusive life. I was taught when I was little that I was different, and that I was a disappointment, because I was born.

NETWORKING

As the little girl hearing it all the time, you start to believe it. Love to me meant pain of one kind or another. I was told I was dumb and different.

My safest place was on the streets. There were some secret places that I found were safe for me. One was in the back of a car lot. There was a cave in a hill leading up to the tracks. I dragged out some old seats, and just made it "my place." I would sit there and wish some things and sing.

Another secret place was in a church under a pew, where I would go and listen to them practice singing. I loved that, and I would sing along. I didn't know it at first, but later learned the priest heard me singing, and knew I was under there. He would sit on a pew and read Genesis. I loved hearing him read, and hearing how the Earth was made. He put a paper bag, with a sandwich and an apple, under the pew.

After a month, I was seen going into church. When I came out, my dad was there. I got hit

THE GLORY PATH

all the way home (four blocks). I remember that I yelled, "You're not going to beat me anymore." Well, he showed me just how bad he can beat me, and he locked me in the attic. That's where my room was for a week.

I ran away as soon as I could get out and lived on the streets. I had to the steal a few times, like clean clothes off someone's clothes line, or soda off a Coke truck (not more than needed). It was one or two bottles to fill my stomach. I went to him later and told him that I took them. He told me not to worry. That's why he left the door open.

I lived in 39 foster homes. I can't say they were all bad. I had a serious trust issue. Now, a few of them didn't want a foster child, they wanted a maid, or the husband thought I was there to play games. I have been raped over seven times before I was 12.

I got into some big fight's just to survive, took some good hits, but gave some too. Not that I like fighting, because I don't like to hurt anyone,

NETWORKING

but I won't run from one either. Once they know you run, they will be at you all the time.

Does this sound like I was a hard person? Yes and no. Inside I wasn't, but outside I had to be.

You see, I forgave so many, but I never could forgive myself (cover it up, yes).

I never trusted to share my true feelings until Steve and his family started the classes on emotional healing, to look way down inside, just free you from the hurts and unforgiveness, with no judgment.

I lived so long being what everybody wanted. Now I am free to be myself. Before this I never cried unless I was cutting an onion. I had learned that crying was weak and some people loved tears. It made them feel strong. But now I learned it is also so refreshing to cry.

Mabel

THE GLORY PATH

TV SHOW, "AMISH OUT OF ORDER"

In the fall of 2011, I received some emails and some phone calls from National Geographic. They were wanting to do a TV show about the Amish. I was not really interested in doing a TV show, so I wasn't immediately responding to the phone calls and emails.

They ended up speaking with one of my brothers, who told them they should get in contact with me. We agreed to meet with the cameraman and a former Amish man off-camera.

During our meeting, we suddenly went into a time of ministry. The cameraman asked us if he can film it and we told him yes.

Since then we have had many people tell us how the show has been a blessing for them, and how it has helped them in their life.

TESTIMONIAL

I found Light of Hope Ministries and Steve Lapp, in a way that some may consider an accident, but I consider it to be God, knowing that He had to use something totally different to get my attention.

NETWORKING

I was sitting in my living room, with the TV on, mindlessly in the background, as I played games on the Internet. It wasn't so much about what was happening on the TV, but how it made me feel, and what I saw in the eyes of Steve Lapp.

I watched that TV episode several times and then I searched the Internet, and read articles, and watched videos, and then I really did something very unlike myself, I made contact with a total stranger.

I didn't find what I expected. I sent challenging messages that were met with honesty and gentleness. I expected to find phony, and I found a realness I could not have imagined. I took verbal swings that were responded to in love.

Through the help of Steve and Light of Hope Ministries, I have been able to let go of years of anger, and I am finding a healing in my heart that I didn't think was possible.

-JB-

A grateful friend in Massachusetts

THE GLORY PATH

WITNESSING TRANSFORMATION

Oh, the wonder of witnessing the transformation that takes place when the peace of Jesus washes away the hate, bitterness, confusion, and unforgiveness!

We felt that we should be able to reach more people than just one or two at a time. We started to do some group counseling (with 10 to 20 people in a group) with awesome results. We are doing more group counseling than one-on-one. It is awesome how open people can be in a group.

On July 23, 2012 our son Melvin Jay was born

"OVERCOMERS COURSE"

The "Overcomers Course" is a five-day group healing, training, teaching and development course. It is designed to help individuals and couples to overcome obstacles in their life and find the freedom and the flow of God's order for their life.

Here are some testimonies as a result of the "Overcomers Course."

NETWORKING

If you take the first letter of each word in that phrase it spells LIGHT OF HOPE you will have:

Love
In
Great
Heaps
That
Opens
Frozen
Hearts
Of
Pain
Excellently

Broken and shattered hearts is a good description of our hearts when we met Light of Hope. We have stepped out in the past and trusted others to care about our issues we were struggling with. There were many who meant well but when the proper knowledge, tools, and love of Jesus were not there, it only deepened and added to the scars that were already in our hearts.

When God lead us to Light of Hope, mainly Steve and Jake, they truly loved us with the love of Jesus and shared the knowledge and tools they had with us. They taught us how to apply the knowledge, tools, and love of Jesus in our everyday lives. The freedom we have found in learning the truth and being set free from satans lies is awesome and has changed our lives.

Sheldon & Tina Burkholder
Myerstown, PA

I grew up in a very dysfunctional home with physical, emotional, and sexual abuse. Because it seemed there was no one to protect me, I developed a very tough girl attitude and did life by my sheer will power. My boiling rage was mostly kept under control, but I was so weary of trying to keep myself together.

Five years ago, I was physically and emotionally exhausted and found myself starting to crash. Instead of starting any antidepressants, I chose to

NETWORKING

look at what was driving the anger in my heart. I knew I was hurting my husband and my children and was desperately looking for something better.

What a boatload of garbage all wrapped in a shell of anger! God sent many people into my life to be 'Jesus with skin-on' until I could even begin to comprehend love from our Father God.

Last year we met Steve and Jake and their families for the first time. Looking back over the past year, I realize it was a divine appointment for us to meet the Light of Hope Ministries team.

When we would meet with Steve and Jake, I was a bit baffled because my anger did not scare them. After a while, I began to feel safe because I could not push them over. They would calmly listen to my pain and never be shocked. One of the biggest things they helped me with was reclaiming my will and power of choice.

THE GLORY PATH

My power of choice was shattered because people in authority sinned against me, so I used anger to propel myself through life. Whenever I was in a difficult situation, I would view myself as the problem, and then boil in anger because I couldn't change everyone around me.

I was suddenly brought up short when Steve remarked, "You are part of the solution of the problem, not the problem itself." What a lovely thought! Deep inside of my heart, I always thought I was the problem, now I choose to be part of the solution.

Now when I find myself resorting to anger I stop and ponder the question, What is a solution to the problem? I then realize I have choices to make. Sometimes I do not like my choices, but I always have a choice. When I realize that I can be part of the solution, my anger starts to dissolve. Also, I am learning how to be empowered by the Holy Spirit instead of resorting to my own will power.

NETWORKING

Another teaching I learned from Light of Hope was the "trash can method" of dealing with injustices that another hurting person may present to us. If I keep my trash can empty by giving my issues to Jesus, I can offer a trash can to others who are hurting me. I can then take their pain to Jesus and not need to take it upon myself, and in turn I am now able to offer them the love of Jesus.

Beyond offering hurting people the love of Jesus, Steve has a gift of working through difficult relationships, and has great teaching on how to bring redemption to broken relationships. I was also shown the importance of forgiveness to those who have hurt me, how to forgive from the heart, and not with my own will power.

Often after a victory and a breakthrough, I would find myself sliding back to where I was previously. Steve helped me see that the enemy was accusing me and wanting me to believe nothing had changed.

THE GLORY PATH

One evening, my husband and I went outside on the stone driveway. After drawing a line with a stick, I boldly declared to the enemy, "I know which side of the line I stand. I will not believe your lies and you cannot tell me that everything is the same."

When I find myself struggling, I go back to the 'line in the sand' and declare my position to the enemy.

In relating to the Light of Hope team, I have felt very honored as a woman. My spiritual gift and my purpose in life was called up and blessed. I was then reminded of it, if I was wallowing in my struggles. I have never felt any insinuation that just because I am a woman I am less spiritual. Instead I was given a place to be a sister warrior against the kingdom of darkness.

Twice I was privileged to take the 'Overcomers Course' that Light of Hope offers. Meeting with a small group of like-minded friends was a great boost. There was teaching, ministry time, and a safe place to belong. I would recommended this course for anyone who wants to know more of God and wants to be empowered for the journey.

My encouragement to everyone is to keep on being an overcomer. If you are facing a difficult situation, keep on facing the enemy. Each small victory will move you towards freedom and light in your heart.

Press on! Raise the banner! Face the foe! We have won the victory!

Marlene Horst
Myerstown, PA

"SHOW ME YOUR WAYS, O LORD, TEACH ME YOUR PATHS."

PSALM 25:4